Assyrian Costumes and Jewelry

Samir Johna and Regina Tower

authorHOUSE®

AuthorHouse™
1663 Liberty Drive
Bloomington, IN 47403
www.authorhouse.com
Phone: 1-800-839-8640

First published by AuthorHouse 2/11/2010

ISBN: 978-1-4490-7404-3 (e)
ISBN: 978-1-4490-7402-9 (sc)
ISBN: 978-1-4490-7403-6 (hc)

Library of Congress Control Number: 2010900298

Printed in the United States of America
Bloomington, Indiana

This book is printed on acid-free paper.

Contents

Prologue

Assyrian Costumes and Jewelry

It is such a wonderful opportunity that two different scholars in specialty, worked together to author this book, an archaeologist and art historian, the late Dr. Walid Al-Jadir, and one of the modern Iraqi painters, Dhia Al-Azzawi. Both had worked in the Iraqi Museum, and know all the details of the Assyrian art from observing the Assyrian sculptures in the museum and in the major Assyrian capitols, Nineveh, Nimrud, Ashur, and Dur Sharrukin (Khorsabad). This nice documentary was finally translated by two scholars in California, Samir Johna, MD, a surgeon by profession and Mrs. Regina Tower, an author and translator, the most qualified persons to do this translating work, because both are Assyrians from Iraq, and both know almost all the details of the Assyrian costumes that they grew with in their early life in northern Iraq.

This work that is now in English is very important, for both the scholars of Mesopotamian archaeology and art history, as well as for the public, it gives all the needed details to track all the costume designs of the Assyrians as well as the textile and the decoration of the costumes, ranging from the costumes of the kings to the ones for the solders and to the normal people in Assyria.

Donny George, Ph.D.
Former Director of the Iraqi Museum
Professor of Mesopotamian Archeology
Stony Brook University, NY

Foreword

It all started on October 4, 2006 when I found myself alone in my contemporary Assyrian costume among ordinary people at Woodbury University, Department of Fashion Design, at Burbank, California. Jean Kardously and Ninos Aho, two Assyrian intellectuals - an inventor and a poet - gave me the impression that an international festival for traditional costumes was underway and the addition of an Assyrian costume would be needed. Instead the event turned out to be a presentation delivered by Dale Gluckman, the former Curator of Costumes and Textiles at the Los Angeles County Museum of Art, entitled," Exotic Inspirations".

The presentation was a unique opportunity for me to learn about something different than my own training as a surgeon, while at the same time it allowed me to introduce my costume to this group of faculty and students who have been, to a certain degree, exposed to ancient Assyrian costumes and jewelry through some sketches Jean had provided as references. The mounting interest in ancient Assyrian designs and fashions is no surprise given that for centuries European and American fashion designers incorporated elements from traditional cultures in the creation of exciting new garments.

Among other references Jean had provided to Woodbury University is an Arabic language original publication of this book in your hand. Jean had accepted it as a gift from a friend who had purchased it in Syria several years ago. The book is, to the best of my knowledge, published by the Ministry of Information Press in Baghdad (Iraq) sometime during the 1970s. The available copy of this now rare book is missing the first four pages, which are in all likelihood outside the core subject.

It has been said that a picture is worth thousand words but the value of the text in this book must not be underestimated. This book reveals and recognizes the contributions of the rich and diverse mastery of the Assyrian artisans of the past. The illustrations taken from the extensive stone relieves from the Neo Assyrian period show the purpose of each item of jewelry and costume and it's relationship to religious, royal, magical, and military specific usage. The garments and jewelry designs have been copied and recopied by many of the societies in eastern and western civilizations. To name a few, the Rogers showrooms in Manhattan traded two varieties of Assyrian flatware patterns; The Assyrian Head introduced in 1886, and the Assyrian introduced in 1887. The Rogers also manufactured hollowware such as pitchers, candy dishes, chargers, tea sets, candlesticks, and items for the table that matched the Assyrian and the Assyrian Head flatware patterns. We learn the origin and reason for the custom that have been adopted time and again in today's culture. Hence I was inspired to take upon myself, and with the assistance of Regina Tower, the task of translating it from Arabic into English. We have researched and interpreted this text so that nothing could be lost in the translation in order to keep its historic and archaeological depth. We hope that this humble contribution allows this valuable but obscure Arabic book from Iraq to enter the collection of items in English that adds to the world culture and allows further appreciation of Iraq's rich Assyrian heritage.

It is worth mentioning that this book addresses the Assyrian costumes and jewelry during the zenith of the Assyrian empire at a time when the Assyrian artisans devoted their time and effort to depict kings, gods, and other dignitaries rather than the public. The archeological discoveries to date suffer paucity of data regarding day to day life of ordinary people. This may in part explain the differences we see in today's costumes compared to the ancient ones. Changes wrought by time, improved manufacturing techniques, and the effects of isolation on most Assyrians- within remote regions of the Middle East due to their ethnic and religious uniqueness that invited persecution, also have affected the somewhat altered designs. Nonetheless, the ancient Assyrian school of arts had left its mark on contemporary costumes of the Middle East, Assyrians and others in terms of colors, embroidery, and elements of decoration, as we will return to elsewhere in this book (see back cover).

To provide a perspective, it is imperative to touch upon the history of present day Assyrians, the indigenous people of Mesopotamia, with a history that goes back to 6759 years. Having ruled the entire Middle East for many centuries, they excelled not only in war but also in peace. Many of their discoveries and inventions are still useful today, speaking for one of the greatest civilizations ever known. In the Assyrian empire lie the origins of the postal system, library collecting, preservation of the Gilgamesh epic, the institution of multi-ethnic political administration and most important of all, spreading writing through use of the first alphabet system, Aramaic, that led to the writing of languages from Mongolian to Hebrew. The letters of the Talmud are still called "Assyrian Letters."

Since the loss of their empire in 612 B.C. Assyrians have been at odds with history. They were the first nation to adopt Christianity in 32 AD, yet through out centuries Christianity became the very cross they had to endure, through one atrocity after another and one genocide after another. Perhaps the worst of all was the forgotten holocaust that befell all Christians of the Middle East under the Ottoman Empire in 1915-1920. Over one million Armenian, two thirds of the entire Assyrian nation, along with Greeks and other Christians, were slaughtered for no reason other than being Christians. The tragedy was relived again, albeit to a lesser extent, in Semele, Iraq in 1933. With over four millions living in over thirty three countries around the globe, the Assyrians have been reduced to a small minority in the Middle East, who are still struggling for existence in their own home land.

In preparing for this book, I had encountered some difficulties, of which getting hold of the authors was the most challenging. Needles to say, the current situation in Iraq did not help. Through a diligent search, I learned that one of the two authors, Walid Al-Jadir, a renowned archeologist, had passed away in Iraq in 1997 after battling cancer. The second author, Dia Al-Azzawi, a renowned artist and archeologist, is currently living in London. His unconditional support through his permission to translate and publish his work was a great impetus for me to proceed as planned and for that I am deeply indebted to him. Securing the permission of the late Walid Al-Jadir, or his representatives, on the other hand, remains a challenge at the present time.

Finally, I would like to thank Dr. Eden Naby of Harvard University and Dr. Donny George of Stony Brook University for their invaluable input and guidance in preparing this book, and Mr. Sargon Younan for his painting on the front cover. This book may become a great source of inspiration to many designers that may want to delve into the fashion world of ancient culture, as well as teachers that would like to trace the origin of western civilization. Written by experts in the field, this book is a must have for any Assyriology students, art historians, and others with a lay or scholarly interest in ancient cultures.

Samir Johna, MD, FACS
Clinical Professor of Surgery
Loma Linda University School of Medicine
Staff Surgeon, Southern California Permanente Medical Group

Basic Introduction in the Study

of the Assyrian Costumes

This research covers the Assyrian costumes and their effect on the appearance of the Assyrians in general. It is appropriate to study the given facts regarding the subject, of which the sculptures are the main source and have the most documental value. However, these sources would not belittle the importance of the Akadian literature in this field.

The expansion and flourishing of the Assyrian empire took place mainly during the Neo Assyrian period i.e. during the reign of kings, Sargon II (721-705 BC), Sennacherib (705-681 BC), Essarhaddon (681-668 BC), and Ashurbanipal (668-626 BC), in addition to other weaker kings who reigned for a few years and had left us no trace or literature to lead to the works or roles they played during that period of time.

The main credit that led to the expansion and flourishing of the empire goes in every aspect to its successful and well organized military campaigns. Through the use of innovative techniques they were able to reach far away countries where their harsh policies were rigorously implemented. In effect, and as expected, the economy of the Assyrian empire flourished by the new sources and resources. These economical changes were reflected in the progress they made in architecture, science, literature, and related fields.

From this period in history, which spans over no more than a century, valuable references are available particularly in the field of literature that was partly original and partly copied from older sources, Sumarian and Babylonian, written on nearly one thousand clay tablets, excluding what was discovered in the library of the Learned Assyrian king Ashurbanipal.

Some of the clay tablets addressed the social status of the royal and the temple artists, and the status of the employed or paid by fee for service independent professional artists. In addition to the per diem professional artists and craftsmen, there was a class of slaves and semi-slaves who after learning a trade, would be enlisted to work at factories that belonged to the royal palaces, the temples, or to work at the homes of the ministers and other dignitaries. The Assyrian kings did not stop at what they had but would bring back to their capitals the best artists of the lands they conquered in addition to those summoned form their own territories when they are needed for large projects. By the same token, artists were occasionally asked to go and help their compatriots in other territories, particularly when it comes to weaving and knitting[1] needed for the royal palaces and the temples.

Our review of the Assyrian literature, records of their transactions and agreements, the exchange letters between the kings and their territorial governors, along with the masterpieces of their vast antiquities, the carved sculptures, metallic pieces made with utmost precision and skill, indicates that the Assyrians were industrial people who practiced and developed the arts of professional trades, which led to the building of healthy and strong economy particularly during the 8th century BC. We also feel that the profound development, which is not attributed only to the spoils the Assyrians seized from their wars, or getting acquainted with the developed industry of the conquered nations, but rather it was mainly due to the fact that the Assyrian ruling class was a productive entity. The growth of their trade and economy led to further increase in productivity and industrial development, as clearly depicted when the variety of their exports to outside their empire peaked during this period especially to the north and to their

---

[1] *It is impossible to point the timing and the exact geographical origin of knitting. Some authorities believe that it started in the pre-Christian era. In personal communication with Dr. Donny George, he indicated that recent discoveries indicate that knitting was known in Mesopotamia in the second century BC.*

commercial colonies in Asia Minor (Cappadoce), particularly in the fields of fabrics, embroidery, and metals.[2]

We must notice that the Assyrian industry and arts were affected by the general status of the Assyrian empire at any given time; as a rule, they progressed in a parallel manner to the political and economical development of the society.

In this research it is important to know that arts served the official needs of the Assyrian empire more than anything else. Excluding some minor arts[3], in general they were not at service of the individuals or the society. The rest were linked directly or indirectly to the royal palace or the temple, particularly costumes and related items[4], major or minor.

The elaborate study of the costumes and their accessories provides the scholars with a clear idea about the human daily life at any given moment in history. The study of the Assyrian costumes is no exception. The Assyrian murals and sculptures from the referenced period provide detailed accounts of the social life in the Assyrian society then. We notice the types of costumes for daily living of the royal society, the costumes of religious festivals, costumes for hunting and war, costumes for the kings to wear when sick or when they want to drive evil spirits away, or to uncover revelations, etc. The murals also depict the tools needed for such occasions.

The study of these murals and sculptures reveals the prim reality that characterized the Assyrian sculptor. This is a sincere reflection for the connection between him (the artist) and the social and psychological

---

[2]   *Carelli P. Les Assyriens en Cappadoce. Paris, 1963.*

[3]   *Crafts used to produce necessary daily utensils.*

[4]   *Farming, raising animal, fleecing, the production of knitting threads from plants such as cotton and linen followed by treatment with chemicals and or colors prior to and after weaving, decoration with jewelry and or embroidery played a complimentary role in giving a new look for the Assyrians costumes characterized by power, splendor, and glory that surpassed the costumes of other nations, which is particularly evident when studying the Greek costumes.*

state of affairs of the Assyrian society; a sincere illustration for the fundamentals of the Assyrian personality[5].

The Assyrian sculptor did not stop at the honest delivery of the social pictures to us but often added natural colors to some body parts and costumes as a complimentary part to the powerful Assyrian looks[6], which was consistent with the initial archeological discoveries in the Assyrian capitals.

The tendency of the Assyrians to use multiple, strong and deep colors did not have a negative effect on their ability to achieve the desired harmony and to emphasize the body lines and the facial features of their kings, known for their power and sternness.

In this capacity, the Assyrian school left its influence on many civilizations. We can easily see this influence on the Islamic arts[7], some elements of which are still prominent today. For example, the tendency to wear embroidered and brightly colored costumes that we see today in northern Iraq is nothing but one example.

The concept of splendor among Assyrians was parallel to what they have achieved in military might and authority that extended as far as southern Egypt, southern Iraq, and Persia. Such features became the defining point for the Assyrian in his exterior appearance.

If we have previously mentioned that costumes served magical connotations, we must know that colors as well played equally important role in affirming such connotations, particularly the white

---

[5]   *Using fresh calcite stone with its known resilience enabled the Assyrian sculptors to achieve the precision they are known for.*

[6]   *Marble and ivory were used to decorate the eyes of some statures; color mix was also used to color head hair and the beards in addition to some costumes; sand paste mixed with green color was used to make pine nuts typically placed in the hands of kings and winged mythical figures as magical symbols.*

[7]   *Will be clarified later in this research.*

and the red[8] along with its related colors, which are derived from plants, animals, and minerals, as supported by a body of literature addressing this subject with precise and intricate details, a subject worth future publications.

The authenticity and the precision by which the Assyrian sculptors reflected the Assyrian features were similar to their ability to reflect the features of non-Assyrian prisoners, their costumes, and even their belongings through a distinction between the various figures on their sculptures. The gods were distinguished from Kings and so were the ministers and servants, through symbols of significance to the Assyrian society.

This period with its advanced arts and industry and the rapid progress made in every aspect of life allows us to look at it as the "period of renaissance" or the "golden era" for the arts of Mesopotamia. The Assyrian school of arts had successfully encompassed the distinctive inclinations and the art attributes of the Medians, Ilamites, and the Phoenicians, along with the Sumerian and the Babylonian effect. They were able to uplift their own concepts in their artistic production after polishing the foreign effects with their pure Assyrian hands. In return, the Babylonians[9] adopted a lot of the elements from the Assyrian school of arts, to inoculate their traditional and classical arts, while marinating their academic inclinations.

The heritage of the Assyrian school of art under our research is nothing but physical evidence to the various exchanged influences that affected the decorative arts to include Jewelry, costumes and their

---

[8]   *The red color and its numerous spectra had many considerations among Assyrians and other contemporary nations, such as illnesses, fending off evil souls, and the use of red cloth when moving to the world of the dead. The white color on the other hand, indicated purity and modesty, thus the costume of the king particularly during religious festivals, and the costume of the clergymen. For more details about these two colors see;*

1.   **Dictionaire Archiologique des techniques. Vol. II, Paris, 1964, p. 600...;**
2.   **Lutz, H.F. Neo-Babylonian Administrative documents from Erech, California, Berkeley, 1927, I, II, p. 85, No. 12...,**
3.   **Forbes, R.J. Studies in Ancient Technology. Vol. IV, Brill Leiden, 1964.**

[9]   *Obviously here we refer to the late or the Neo-Babylonian period.*

adornment. We must notice that there was no one regional art, or one territorial civilization but rather various civilizations exchanging influence in the midst of the ability of each nation to immortalize its attributes in the field of arts and industry.

The historians of art simulate the arts of Mesopotamia during ancient times to a tree that continued to grow vigorously while remained strong and deeply rooted from the beginning.

The Akhminians had adopted the civilization of their neighbors to a point it is safe to say that the same Assyrian and Babylonian elements and subjects had been transferred and nearly adopted and implemented to the east, particularly Persia. The wealth of the Persian kings —much like the Assyrians- was reflected by the luxurious antiquities they left behind as best depicted by the magnificently colored engravings on the walls of their vast palaces representing their daily royal living.

There is an obvious similarity between the subjects of these engravings and the subjects addressed by the Assyrians on the costumes and the adornments. The elements of the Assyrian decorative arts were apparent on the engravings for the cities of Sus, and Persipolis, as well as the palace of King Darius and his magnificently decorated sculptures in exhibition today at the British museum.[10]

If the Akhminians and others who came into contact with Mesopotamian civilization could not refuse the premier rich, and deeply rooted heritage of the Assyrian civilization, they also enjoyed new artistic elements from Ararto of the north, and Ilam of the south, which was already influenced by the Sumerian and Babylonian civilizations, particularly during the reign of the Babylonian king Hammurabi. We must not forget the influence of the decorative elements that the Akhminians copied from some nomadic groups such as the Sethians

---

[10]   Barnett, R.D Les Reliefs des palais Assyriens, Praque, 1959, p. 24-25.
      Barnett, R.D. Iraq. XiX (1957) " Pesipolis" bas-relief : Pls : XV3, XIX, I, V, XX, XXI, 4.

and the Simarians[11] although some believe that the Armenians were the main vehicle of transport to the Akhminians.

Then was the role of the Sassanides who carried their arts to the west during their quick expansions, which encompassed the artistic elements of the territories they had captured. As such they played the link between the preceding civilizations that flourished in this region and the new civilizations, i.e. the Islamic civilization followed by the European medieval civilization, which makes whoever wants to study the Islamic costumes and fabrics compelled to study its Sassanide as well as the Coptic and the Byzantine counterparts. Here we must mention that some historians tried to favor the Coptic influence and considered them the first masters of the Islamic school of arts and what came earlier. However, this opinion lacks accuracy since it is clear and known that the Islamic artists found the Coptic fabrics only a reflection of their taste that goes in harmony with their geometrical decorations and formations, which are mostly calligraphic decorations. Other than that, the influence of the Sassanides had the upper hand upon the artists of the Islamic era, i.e. every thing pertaining to subject, decoration of fabrics, and colors, i.e. what creates a close spiritual atmosphere attributed to the wandering nomadic spirit that the Islamic artists had lived, the long wars that they went through, and what came from hunting in terms of experience and wisdom. We can see the outcome clearly echoed in their productions. Furthermore, it is only logical to study the roots of these Islamic influences and their effects in the areas the Muslims occupied and came into contact with before other places. Here we mean Persia, where at first the Muslims were able

---

[11]   *People of Persian origins who came to Persia from southern Russia via the Kavkaz. The Sethians were mentioned in the Greek sources, particularly in the writings of Herodotus, in the Assyrian texts, and in the Torah as Asikoza. In the 8th century B.C., the Sethians and the Simarians simultaneously raided western Asia. Being hostile tribes, they were able to reach from Kavkaz to Palestine and from Ararto to southern Persia. However, they were forced to retreat to the north of Kavkaz at the turn of the 6th century B.C. for more details see;*

1.   **Ghirshman, R. Parthes et Sassanides, Paris, 1962.**
2.   **Ghirshman, R. Les Achemenides, Paris, 1963.**
3.   **Ghirshman, R. L'Iran, Des origines a L'Islam, Paris, 1951.**

to enlist experienced artists and the labor required. Later such resources were enlisted from Egypt. Finally, they also acquainted themselves with various art samples from Mesopotamia, Syria, Byzantine.

The flourishing, expansion and dispersion of the Persian arts left an influence on the Coptic artists and weavers. Often times, we find Sassanide decorative forms in the products of the Coptic weavers, and occasionally Byzantine decorative elements as well. Among the most prominent Sassanide forms in the Coptic weaving products that reflect a special sanctity is the display of animal facing each other on either side of a prayer niche, a fire, a life tree, or a sacred tree. All these elements played a role not only among Sumerians, but in all Mesopotamian civilizations, particularly among Assyrians in their late period, which was widely used by the Byzantines before they found their way to Arabic and Islamic decorations.

An important phase that followed was the era of Alexander and the new relations with the conquered east this time. This phase is characterized by the trend to go back and adopt the elements of prior phases. However, we notice that adopting and imitating favored less intricacy and intensification as compared to the Assyrian era particularly the art of decorating costumes on the murals with complex, luxurious jewelry. Never the less, these tendencies were not distant from the formations and the symbols of the preceding phases.

This attempt to review the Assyrian costumes industry requires mentioning that the Assyrian murals did not favor recording aspects of the Assyrian public in life (laborers, soldiers, etc.) as they emphasized the simplicity in their costumes as we will address later.

It is important to record that the Assyrian murals are unique in the tyrannical absence of women while it was not the case on the cylinder seals prevalent then. This absence was not random but rather a reflection for the Assyrian stance on women, which is reflected in the laws they enacted.

The Industry of the Assyrian Costumes

The Costumes of the Kings, the

Clergy, and the Royal Retinue

The external appearance of the kings, the clergy and the royal retinues is composed of two pieces: the first piece is the tunic which varies in length, and is often embroidered and adorned in traditional forms and designs that can also bee seen on the outer garments. The second piece is the cloak, which is usually worn directly over the tunic. Contrary to the tunic, the cloak can not be worn by itself[12].

The cloak was clearly seen worn by the Assyrians and for the first time towards their middle reign and during the first millennium BC. Its use was limited to the gods and kings to be distinguished from others displayed on the Assyrian murals[13]. The cloak reaches down to below the knees. It opens in the front or both sides or on one side only, ending on its lower end with fringes [14]in continuation with the garment. The fringes are part of weaved fabric and not an additional piece.

---

[12]   *Those who want to search the Assyrian costumes must study the use of the raw materials in the industry, which has been documented in the Acadian literature, such as wool that was the main resource in the industry; the linen on the other hand was mainly used for making the clothing of the clergymen; the cotton which was introduced into Mesopotamia for the first time by king Sennacherib (also called the tree that carries wool), and some other materials used on limited scale such as hemp and leather.*

[13]   *In addition to other essential differences in the designs and symbols.*

[14]   *Called "Sharashib" in Iraqi dialect and is used for whatever hangs loose. See our article:*
   1.   **The buttons. Al-Turath Al-Sha'abi, Part I, 1968, p. 23.**

The royal cloaks and those specific for gods were decorated at the chest area with elements of adornments in religious and mythical themes, executed with colorful embroidery in addition to the frequent use of gold and silver threads. Often times they were decorated with jewelry and colored precious stones, which were well known to them[15].

Before we go into details, we like to emphasize the significance of costumes among Assyrians. In Mesopotamia costumes symbolized many subjects, particularly among Assyrians. Some costumes were reserved for certain occasions, others had to be cleaned at certain times and dates.

Ceremonial letters and those related to witchcraft, fortune telling and prophesies provided detailed information about such ceremonies, in which costumes played a vital role. In a letter text from the era of the Assyrian king Essarhaddon (681-668 BC) we find the sender begging the king to send him two clergymen to help in a religious ceremony related to costumes before it was too late[16]. In another text, we find the details of a royal costume[17].

"… In regards to the white costume that my lord referred to in his letter asking how many days I have to wear them? Let my lord wear them on the 20th and the 21st of the month. Two days are enough and on 22nd day the sleeves of the tunic will become sacred. I hope my lord and master will follow the routine.

---

[15] *For more details, see:*
   1. **Boson, G. Les Metaux et les pierres dans les inscriptions assyrio-baby-loniennes, Munchen, 1914; Scheil V. Revue d'Assyriologie. XV, p. 122.**
   2. **Thompson C. Dictionary of Assyrian Chemistry and Geology. Oxford, 1936, p. 133.**
   3. **Von Soden. Akkadisches Handworterbuch, Wiesbaden, p. 530.**
   4. **The Assyrian Dictionary of the Oriental Institute of the University of Chicago, Gluckstadt. Vol. IV, p. 108.**

[16] **Waterman, L. Royal Correspondence of the Assyrian Empire, 1930, Let: 496, 667.**

[17] *Contrary to the Ancient Egyptian belief, the Assyrian king is not god. He is a war leader, the commander of the Assyrian military divisions, the great and capable king; the king of Assyria.*

The white costumes[18], always made from linen, held a special religious status and were limited to the prominent clergymen during religious ceremonies. Rarely, the kings wore them on special occasions[19].

The production of these costumes from linen was accompanied by certain rituals, legends, and folklore singing unique to Mesopotamia from its early ages[20].

It was also common among the clergymen of Egypt and the Hebrews and in many books of the Torah we find a reference to the white costumes in specific religious rituals[21]. All considered linen a symbol of spiritual purity and many civilizations were influenced by such concept. Linen pieces and linen ribbons were also used to decorate headwear such as turbans and crowns decorated with jewelry, or to the periphery of certain garments.

On the royal costumes and their rituals we find in other letters a text describing how the king should had wore strange costumes to complete a specific religious ritual. It described how the king had to wear a pregnant female costume and in another ceremony he had to wear only a long white garment or a cloak loaded with appropriate jewelry. Occasionally we find that the king must wear some rough garments intended for the guilty and those seeking repentance.

In another document describing such ceremonies and festivals, one Assyrian king was carrying oblation to god Shamash. It also indicates that on the 20th day of the month[22], the king himself offered food in white garments to god Shamash.

---

[18]   *See footnote on page 4.*

[19]   *Mentioned in some texts related to dressing rituals without further details.*

[20]   **Van Dijk, J.J.A. La Sagesse Sumero-accadienne, recherches sur les genres litteraires des textes sapientiaux, avec choix des textes. Leiden, Brill, 1953**

[21]   *See :*
Jacques Lourd. Le Lin et l'industrie Liniere. Paris, que sais-je ?, 1964 ; p. 10... ; L'Exode : 1-31.

[22]   *The year was divided by the lunar system into 12 months. Occasionally an additional month is added for balance with the solar year. Every month was divided into 29 or 30 days. The first months starts with the new appearance of the moon. All these days and months were dedicated to specific gods attached to specific stars or planets through specific symbols.*

The importance that the Assyrians had placed on costumes can be emphasized by the fact that costumes occasionally represented the king at religious festivals when he was confined at his palace due to bad omen or due to possible dangers of wars, etc. When such representation takes place, the senior clergy would complete the rituals in front of the complete royal costume to include the headwear, the jewelry, and whatever completes the festive royal costume. Some available texts detail this interesting subject. In one such text dating to king Essarhaddon when the letter sender requests an order from his king to send his costumes to the location of the festival, on which words will be read related to religious rituals. Another text draws the king's attention to the coming of god Sin on the 17th day when he should go to the house of the festival, and he was advised to send his costumes so that god Sin may chant the religious songs over them and to bless his reign. Most of these texts date back to the late Assyrian era[23].

The Assyrian literature shows that there are many types of festive costumes. The most important one was called 'Kozito" which was worn only by the gods, kings, and the grand clergymen.

This attire, in its external appearance displays all the royal splendor, luxury, and greatness, similar to what is seen during official and religious festivals of Medieval Europe. The outer cloak was the symbol of royalty. When worn by the king, the attire symbolizes the divine nature of the king according to the Assyrian and Mesopotamian beliefs. The Kozito on the other hand signifies the hereditary nature of the throne[24].

There are many types of festive and religious attires described in the Assyrian literature and are depicted on the sculpted murals.

---

23   *See:*

1.   **Waterman, L. Royal Correspondence of the Assyrian Empire, University of Michigan, 1930, IV, Vols.**

2.   **Pfeiffer, R. State Letters of Assyria, New Haven, 1935.**

3.   **Labat, R. Le Caractere religieux de la royaute assyriobabylonienne. 2 vols. Paris, 1939.**

24   **Waterman, L. Royal Correspondence of the Assyrian Empire. Letter No. 870.**

Most of these attires were decorated with gold and silver metallic threads, and with jewelry forged in different sizes[25] or shapes such as a star with multiple formations, flowers, or squared, rectangular, cylindrical formations as will be alluded to later. All these pieces were hung to the clothes using metal threads, so as they could be removed for cleaning or repair. The buttons, on the other hand, were considered decorative jewelry in addition to their main purpose.

The excavations of the French explorer Victor Place at Khorsabad (Dur-Sharrukin) confirmed that these buttons were used to decorate the royal military suits and military suits of the commanders as well as the famous reins of their horses known as being unique among the horses of the ancient civilizations[26].

---

[25]   *The size of the jewelry reflected the social and religious status of the owner. Such paraphernalia belonged to kings and gods only when used with the crown.*

[26]   *The Assyrians were known for their interest in the appearance of their horses including the saddles that were similar in weaving to the marvelous mural decorative rugs. We think they covered their saddles with a thin weave of linen. For additional information see the research about the rugs and the methods of decoration among the Assyrians in the manuscript about the handicrafts during the Assyrian Era by Walid Al-Jadir, Ph.D.*

The Headwear

The headwear represents an important complimentary element of the Assyrian attire. In general, it points to divine and religious symbols in accordance to the ancient Mesopotamian myths. The fabric headwear was among the royal symbols placed before the gods during the Festive God Assembly in the sky. This symbolized the connection between gods and the mortal human. Excluding that of the clergymen, the headwear was usually decorated with symbols or other decorative formations.

Therefore there is a strong connection between god and these holy symbols. For example, the crown that is placed over the king's head during coronation is considered the great and the magnificent crown of god Ashur, the grand Assyrian god.

God Sin – the god of the moon- is the god of the crown, and the moon light is the body of the crown. When the moon is crescent, it is viewed as a face with two horns, the face of a small strong bull with tough and solid horns. They were considered the symbols of divinity. The horns were essential elements for the crown along with the shiny and glittering beams. Thus, light and glitter held an important place among Assyrians, and became fundamental elements of divinity and monarchy[27].

---

[27] *See the translations of the various Assyrian texts regarding this subject by Elena Cassin. La Splendeur divine. See also;*

    1. **Von Soden. Akkadisches Handworterbuch, p. 643, "Melammu".**

    2. **Waterman, L. Royal Correspondence of the Assyrian Empire, No. 1455...**

    3. **Walid Al-Jadir. Introduction and critique to the La Splendeur, Summer, 23, 1968.**

This is why the Assyrians exaggerated-in accordance with their religious beliefs- the use of glittering precious stones and gold in decorating the headwear and the costumes.

It was the persona of the god or the king that gave the illuminating and the majestic power to the jewelry. Before this divine power, no human could come close to the god or the king else he or she would be overpowered by just looking or gazing at them.

Thus the crown and the jewelry symbolized the whole power, divine and monarchic. We know that goddess Ninmena is the lady and the goddess to the crown for whom the rituals were established and sacrifices were presented to her and to god Anu on daily basis, particularly at the city of Warka.

The turban and the crown were low to start with but gradually grew in height and assumed a conical shape. In general, they were formed in tiers decorated with same decorations used for the costumes in addition to some unique decorative ribbons.

The turban shaped headwear belonged to the clergymen class. It symbolized the religious divinity and monarchy. The marvelous bands that hanged down the headwear had no religious significance. They were often added to the front or the back of the crown or the turban, the loose end of which were mostly decorated with fringes or with jewelry in the shape of a flower.

The headwear, when first decorated with bands, a single band was used. As time went by, more bands were added. The shape and the form of the turban and the crown progressed by the addition of the tiers and the decorative formations, particularly for the crown that turned into the shape of incomplete cone. To its upper part, a pear shaped, structure decorated with ornaments is added. The crown of the king Asurbanipal (626-668 BC) with its five tiers decorated with flowers and various decorative ornaments is the most magnificent example.

The basic materials used in making the headwear were mostly linen and wool. Rarely the silk was used. They were dyed with rare and expensive colors such as the purple in its different shades, and the blue.

The Assyrian literature alluded to double crowns. In a text dating back to the Ashurbanipal era, we read:

"...in the temple of Harran[28], we find the god Sin carrying a rod and wearing a double crown."

Other texts referred to god Anu carrying this divine crown. We find in a text of a letter about the religious rituals a mention of it:

"...it is a must to carry four loaves of bread before the double crowns of god Anu."

And in a letter addressed to the Assyrian king Essarhaddon, the decorations of the headwear of the god Anu, the god of the sky was described:

"...the cylindrical seals handed to me by my lord the king are fit to be used as precious stones to decorate the crown of the god Anu. As to your stones, they are fit cylindrical decorations."

Another letter describes the decorations:

"...according to the old model, I remade the golden crown decorated with precious stones, which must be placed on a bench or platform made of gypsum....and...[29]is placed before my lord god Shamash.[30]"

---

[28]   *Harran, an important city in Mesopotamian cultural and religious heritage, is located today in upper Mesopotamia (South East Turkey). It was the city where Asur Ablat declared himself the Assyrian knig after the fall of Nineveh in 612 BC. The god Sin was so sacred among the Assyrians that the kings dedicated their offspring to become clergy for him.*

[29]   *The interruption refers to a break in the tablet.*

[30]   *God Shamash is the god of the sun and the illuminator of both the upper and the lower worlds. It has been depicted with light beams coming out of its shoulders. He is the god that makes the day and the night, provides life, resurrects the dead, and is the god of justice, rightness, and codes.*

Costumes of the Royal

Retinue and the public

We must, after speaking about the costumes of the kings, the gods, and the clergymen, provide some brief words about the costumes of the royal retinue and the public.

When we say royal retinue, it means the ministers, army commanders, and women. The public includes the soldiers, laborers, and the artists.

The costumes of the ministers are similar to those of the kings except for being not as splendid when it comes to the decorative use of the metals, jewelry, and the precious stones. The importance of the headwear among the Assyrians dictates a unique style for that of the ministers. It is usually no more than a piece of cloth surrounding the head, and covering half of the forehead. The hair is usually visible from top and generally lacks decorations.

The outfit of the Assyrian warrior[31] differs according to the ranks and the specialty. The outfit of the soldiers and other lower ranks in the Assyrian army is no more than a tunic that did not go beyond the knees except for the royal guards, and the archers and what is related to them. The soldier outfit lacks the decorations except for the waist belt that carried some humble decorations.

High ranking officers and commanders of the Calvary tended to dress elegantly. However, the costumes remained somewhere between those of the public and the king and gods. Their military ranks, however, were distinguished by two things; the headwear and the nature of the decorations on the outfit. By them you can distinguish the army

---

[31] *The details of these costumes are outside the scope of this research.*

commander from the hero of the palace, from the master of the city, and from the camp commanders[32] ...etc.

As to women, their appearance on the sculpted murals is extremely rare[33] reflecting the fact that the Assyrian society was sheer masculine to a point they did not care about her absence[34].

This is corroborated by the texts discovered in the Assyrian capitals addressing social and legal matters, which contained only two paragraphs directly outlining the social standing of women in the Assyrian society. They stipulated that married women and the girls of free fathers must wear a veil exposing no more than the face when out on the streets. Female slaves and adulterers must stay unveiled with no veil over her head. If a pedestrian spots otherwise, he must detain the violator and hand her over to courts where she is usually sentenced to fifty lashes in addition to pouring asphalt on her head[35]. As to the queen's costume, we can provide some information by describing the costume of queen Ashursharrat sitting before her husband king Ashurbanipal wearing a tunic reaching to her feet. The sleeves reach just above the wrists decorated with unique embroidery. On her shoulders there is a broad shawl decorated with small circular pieces of jewelry. The tunic and the shawl end with dense fringes. The most important aspect of Naqia's costume (king Essarhaddon's mother) is the crown. In a bronze engraving discovered recently, it appeared very similar to that of Ashursharrat from the described scene above[36].

To complete the picture we think it is important to give a brief description of what is left, the costumes of the laborers and the artists, which were extremely similar on the sculpted Assyrian murals and

---

[32]   *These ranks are literal translations for Assyrian military terms.*

[33]   *We do not find on the Assyrian sculpted murals any women that can be of use for the study of the female costume except for Ashurbanipal's wife (Ashursharrat) and (Naqia) the mother of king Essarhaddon.*

[34]   *In contradiction to the ancient Egyptians, who depicted woman freely and frequently to the point she surpassed the male figure in many cases.*

[35]   *It is not known if the contemporary use of the phrase "ashes on your head" as a symbol of shame among Assyrians of today is related to this notion.*

[36]   **Parrot, A. Assur. Paris, 1961, Fig : 60, 133.**

somewhat similar to the costumes of the soldiers and the low ranks warriors. Usually humble costumes no more than short sleeved tunics, which rarely go beyond the knees with occasional simple decorations, and colorful ornaments on the edges. Finally, many of the laborers were depicted in scenes revealing the cruelty of the work they performed.

According to what we have mentioned earlier concerning the interest of the Assyrian kings in their luxurious and splendid appearance, we must say a few words about a complimentary part of the general royal attire in his processions, the royal umbrella.

The royal umbrella symbolized monarchy and divinity and was not just for the usual need of the umbrella that we know today. It symbolized the king's glory, his good deeds and his flourishing rule. They believed that whoever enjoyed its shade enjoyed the prestige and the protection of the king.

The royal umbrella is sheer Assyrian for it was the only nation that had used it among the neighboring nations.

The purpose was not the mere protection of the king. From the back, a long piece of cloth was added for better shade, particularly during Sargon's era. The umbrella is usually made of a good weave with rare and expensive colors set in with the usual embroideries. In texts from the era of king Sargon the second, they were described as being decorated with gold jewelries.

The Assyrian Goldsmithery

Before we move to the subject of the belts, it is appropriate to say a few words about the art of goldsmithery among the Assyrians. The Assyrian documentary writings did not ignore the smiths, their raw materials and the names of some of their tools.

These documents[37] tell us about types of metals, their degree of glitter, particularly the gold. Many letters documented the abundance of gold in different forms and colors that was dedicated for making decorative elements. It is known that the use of jewelry for costume decorations was known in Mesopotamia before the Assyrians. One text alluded that 700 gold flowers along with the dress made to be decorated, weighted 11.5 kg, the costume of god Nana. In another text, 6 kg of a unique gold was dedicated to make flowers for the costumes of god Sarpanit[38].

Most of the gold in hold of the smiths came from the stores of the palace. We do not have a complete and convincing understanding of the techniques employed by the Assyrian smiths. The available texts provide incomplete information. Further more, the continuous excavations yielded no additional information pertaining to this subject. We do know that the Assyrians had had some renowned artists who crafted very intricate arts in spite of the lack of advanced tools required for such tasks. We know that they were skillful in cutting the gold[39] and

---

[37]   **Garreli, P. Historie general du travail, p. 67.**
     Limet, H. Le travail du metal au pays de Sumer au temps de la IIIe dynastie d'Ur. Paris

[38]   **Waterman, L. Letter No. 498.**

[39]   *Victor Place, a French explorer, discovered golden tree leaves which maintained their intricate lines and roots in spite of the long land effects.*

other metals, along with engraving. They were also skillful in melting, mixing, and many other crafts[40].

What is important in this field is to know if ironsmithery took a complimentary role with goldsmithery in executing the decorative formations.

---

[40] *For more details, see:*

1. **Waterman, L. Royal Correspondence of the Assyrian Empire, 4 Vols. 1930.**
2. **Dictionnaire archeologique des techniques. Tom: II, Paris, 1964.**
3. **Oppenheim, L. Journal of the Near Eastern Studies. Chicago, VIII, 1948.**
4. **Garelli, P. Historie general du travail. Paris, 1959.**
5. **Forbes, R.J. Studies in Ancient Technology, Vol. VIII, Leiden. Brill, 1964.**

Belts

The tunic is often tied with a belt (Hzano)[41]. Literature indicates several types of belts that were usually made of wool or linen. The term symbolized the belts of goddesses and women and was considered specific to god Shamash. Another term used for belts was "Asiho", which were usually made of wool and dyed in azure-blue.

The Assyrians considered the belts to be a sublime and prestigious decorative element thus larger in size than usual to give the weavers the flexibility to execute various adornments and embroideries. A wide strap was usually added to the top of the belt for carrying up to three swords. It was also used for decoration as it extended to above the shoulder like a shawl. Occasionally decorative straps hanged from the belt all the way to below the knees. The belts also symbolized monarchy since the Assyrian kings held the belts as a proof to their power and grandeur. Among Babylonians, on the other hand, belts were part of the clergymen costumes, from which the Hebrews borrowed as symbols and decorations.

The belt of the sensual goddess Ishtar was considered a sacred wear. The untying of a belt among two people was an open invitation for sexual interaction. Therefore religious marriages between the clergyman-king representing the divine broom and the clergywomen representing the divine bride entailed the untying of the belt in between them as a symbol for marriage between male and female. The Greek and

---

[41]   *No wonder that the belt in Acadian "Hzano" is close its Arabic counterpart (Hzam) being both Semitic languages.*

the Roman civilization had adopted this custom from Mesopotamia whether in symbolic or in conceptual manner[42].

The belt also had some religious connotations. One cuneiform text from Ras-Shamra (Ugarit)[43] refers to how to present a belt as a sacrifice to goddess Ishtar. Here we find the goddess depicted in long gown in the shape of tunic with buttons in front and tied with a belt around the waist[44].

According to the ritual protocol of presenting sacrifices in such ceremonies the husband unties his wife's belt. The wife takes off her gown and throws it while holding it behind her with one hand, exposing the beauty of her complete nudity. Thus we find goddesses depicted on some cylinder seals named the nude goddesses[45].

Some Babylonian and Assyrian texts point to many unions between gods, such as the union between god Enki and Ninhursag[46]. In addition there is another text point to how king Sargon (721-705 BC) untied the belt of goddess Ishtar:

"… Oh! The daughter of god Sin be patient and lenient in your residence. Bless Sargon the guard of Assyria, who is walking behind you, he is holding onto your belt."[47]

---

[42]   *This concept was known among ancient Chinese. Its sexual connotation is also known among current nomads of Iraq – as far as we know – indicating that in the beginning humans used the belts to cover their privates in addition to a tool for carrying utilities and weapons. It progressed thereafter to what looks like a short skirt.*

[43]   *An area at the current Syrian-Iraqi borders that was occupied in the past by mixed Semitic people.*

[44]   **Parrot, A. Studia Marina. Fig: 12, p. 32.**

[45]   **Contenau, G. Deesse nue. Fig : 101 et 36.**

[46]   **Kramer, S.N. Mythe Sumerien d'Enki et de Ninhursag. I, p. 241-250.**

[47]   **Craig, J.A. Assyrian and Babylonian Religious Texts. Vol. I, 1895, PI: 54-56=K: 3600.**

Objects of Decorations

We dedicated this chapter to objects of decorations because of the importance of decoration in the Assyrian costumes and the religious, mythical, and social symbols it held.

The "sacred tree" in its various formations, standing alone, or in the presence of mythical or natural animals on both sides dominated other subjects because it represented an essential element in religious rituals, not only for the Assyrians but also for the Babylonians as well. It was attached to worship of the grand god, which is often depicted with the sacred tree above him.

The phenomenon of drawing animals on both sides of the tree (with its religious and decorative symbol) had a tremendous influence on the people of the region, particularly the Hebrews. The book of Exodus (28, 33) refers to decorating the costumes of Aaron before he presented in front of the Lord:

"… And Aaron shall bear the judgments of the children of Israel upon his breast before the Lord continually. And you shall make the robe of Ephod[48] all in blue. And there shall be an opening in the top of it, in the midst thereof; and it shall have a binding of woven work round about the opening of it, hemmed on the edge so that it may not be torn. And on the hem of it you shall make pomegranates of blue and of purple and of scarlet round about the hem thereof; and bells of gold shall be between them round about. A golden bell and a pomegranate, on the hem of the robe round about. And it shall be upon Aaron when he ministers; and its sound shall be heard when he enters the holy place before the Lord and when he comes out, that he may not die.…"

---

[48] *Refers to a sacred dress made of helical threads of golden linen and colored in purple and blue.*

The liberal use of golden pomegranates in decorating the branches of the sacred tree by the Assyrians and their use to decorate the ends of their dresses in the form of embroidery was the impetus for the Hebrews to decorate Aarons' robe as described.

The sacred tree can be in various forms. It can be no more than unlimited lines in number and direction to reflect the branches. Some times the branches terminate at a pomegranate or a pear or any other fruit, in different sizes or forms. All of them had symbolic connotations, mostly religious in nature. The best example is the one embroidered on the outer garment of the tunic of the Assyrian king Ashurnasirpal the second (883-853 BC). The sculpted murals from the era of this king are rich in marvelous and intricate engravings, particularly of the sacred tree, with two animals, one on each side, sitting on their hind legs in a symbolic position, an epitome for the opulence of the palm tree. Occasionally the animals are depicted with horns or with wings, or depicted with their heads directed backwards[49].

There were many animals that were embroidered on the royal robes and on the cylindrical seals in a similar formations dating back to the same era. Among others, there were four goats, two on each side of the sacred tree facing each other[50].

In another scene we find embroidered date palms in addition to the sacred tree on the royal robe of the Assyrian king Ashurnasirpal the second. The fruit of the sacred tree this time is in the form of pine cone shaped as a pear. We may also find the mythical winged persona holding in their left hands small vessels similar to old Iraqi buckets filled with sacred water, and in their right hands male clusters touching the margins of the branches of the female tree, It is favored that these

---

[49]   *See:*

1.   **Budge, E.A. Assyrian Scriptures in the British Museum, reign of Asurnasirpal. London, 1914.**

2.   **Perrot, G. et Chipiez, Ch. Historie de l'art dans l'antiqquite. II, Paris, 1884.**

[50]   **Iraq. XVII (1955), p. 99, pl, XII.**

mythical persona represented the winds that carry the fertilizing pollens from a tree to another[51].

Among the objects that the Assyrian embroiders had executed on the royal robes is the lion, the symbol of power and vitality, wrestling or attacking a unicorn animal depicted in legs of an ox. The lion played a significant role in the myths of Mesopotamian people of different civilizations.

The extreme interest of the Assyrian artist in lions was the impetus for them to dissect them in order to maximize their ability to feature the lions on sculptures.

The pursuit and close observation in owe and bewilderment of lions by the Assyrian artists helped them render marvelous pictures of these animals and their movements in different positions. The Assyrian emphatic endeavor in showing the lions on their mural engravings reflects their great interest, specially the kings, in these animals. The sincere motions seen on the sculpture of the wounded lioness and the scenes of hunting lions are nothing but examples for their deep affection for them.

Among other embroidered scenes, we find dears in different forms along with different plants, scenes of ostriches and other wild animals.

When observing the embroidered piece on chest of King Asurnasirpal's (668-626 BC) gown, we find originality, precision in work and art that knew no match through out Mesopotamian civilizations.

Five tiers were embroidered with different jewelry. Two Indian lotus flowers and the Assyrian flower[52] were located at the center of the embroidered piece of the chest to involve the three central tiers. The

---

[51] **Labat, R. La Caractere religieux de la royaute Assyro-babylonienne. Paris, Tom. II, 1939, p. 289.**

[52] *Also known as the diamond spring flower.* See **Dictionary of plant names by Ahmad Essa Beg, Cairo, 1926, 30, 13.**

forth tier was embroidered with flowers[53]. The fifth tier was divided into small squares.

It appears that the Assyrian sculptor strives, as it appears to us, to create a connection between the king's costumes and his surroundings. To make our point, we take for example the persona of the warrior standing to the left of the monarch Asurbanipal. His outfit gives the impression of a tapestry and its intricate decorations. We see it embroidered with lines of squares with small circles in the centers, followed by other lines decorated on the inside by overlapping lines.

These elements of decoration are well known to be original for the Assyrians[54]. The artists of the neighboring nations could not have admired, ladled and adopted from the contemporary Assyrian and Babylonian arts more, particularly the Phoenicians. In the book of Joshua (7, 21) is written:

"... When I saw among the spoils a beautiful Babylonian tapestry and two hundred shekels of silver and a wedge of gold weighing fifty shekels, then I coveted them and took them; and, behold, they are hidden in the earth inside of my tent, and the silver under it."

It is worth documenting that the Assyrians maintained the forms and the unity of the unique objects of decoration during the entire era of king Sargon without overt change.

Our final word here is that the subject of the Assyrian costumes and their connotations is an extensive and important topic in the research of Mesopotamian civilizations that a book like ours is unable to cover adequately, but it is a humble attempt to establish and confirm

---

[53]　*The decorations were not limited to costumes and jewelries but extended to architecture to fill the gaps in scenes of mural engravings, the decorations for the handles of swords and rods, and even the shoes.*

[54]　*In his excavations at the Assyrian capitals in the first part of the nineteenth century, the British explorer Henry Layard discovered many items of decoration. Some were small cylinders decorated from within by small circular tiers diverging from the same center, i.e. helical, while others were decorated by formations of rhomboid lines and spiky edges, or parallel or decussating lines, or bands in similar formation. All were known to the Assyrians. See* **Layard, H. Discoveries in the Ruins of Nineveh and Babylon. II Volumes, London 1853.**

some precise documentation. Here it is possible to add that factories of weaving and knitting fabrics and the skillful Assyrian and Babylonian embroiders made Mesopotamia famous among the nations of the ancient world, and through which the Assyrian fabrics decorated with gold pieces and colored threads became known as the golden costumes due to the extensive application of such fabrics, particularly gold by the Assyrians and the Babylonians. This was clearly documented by the Greek writers and the earlier sources.

Finally, the softness of their fabrics and their pleats revived architecture and minimized the rigidity and the monotony inherent in rigid fabrics. It also added to wall engraving and the entire architecture a permanent atmosphere of festivity.

Assyrian Costumes and Jewelry

The Sketches

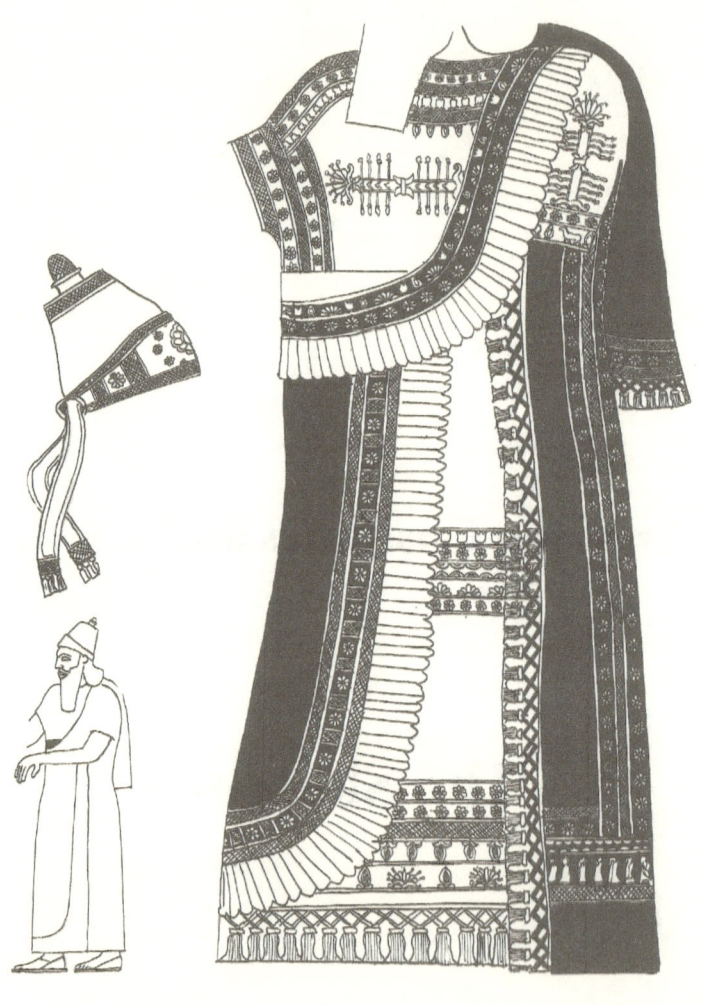

Ceremonial costume of king Ashurnasirpal (1050-1032 BC) See the decorative formations of the entire gown including the shawl. The sacred tree decorating the front of the tunic and the upper arms in embossed embroidery is among the most popular decorations, particularly in the chest area. This era represent the most resourceful period for the study of Assyrian costumes and their decorations.

Layard, A. H. The Monuments of Nineveh, Volume 2, Pl: 34.

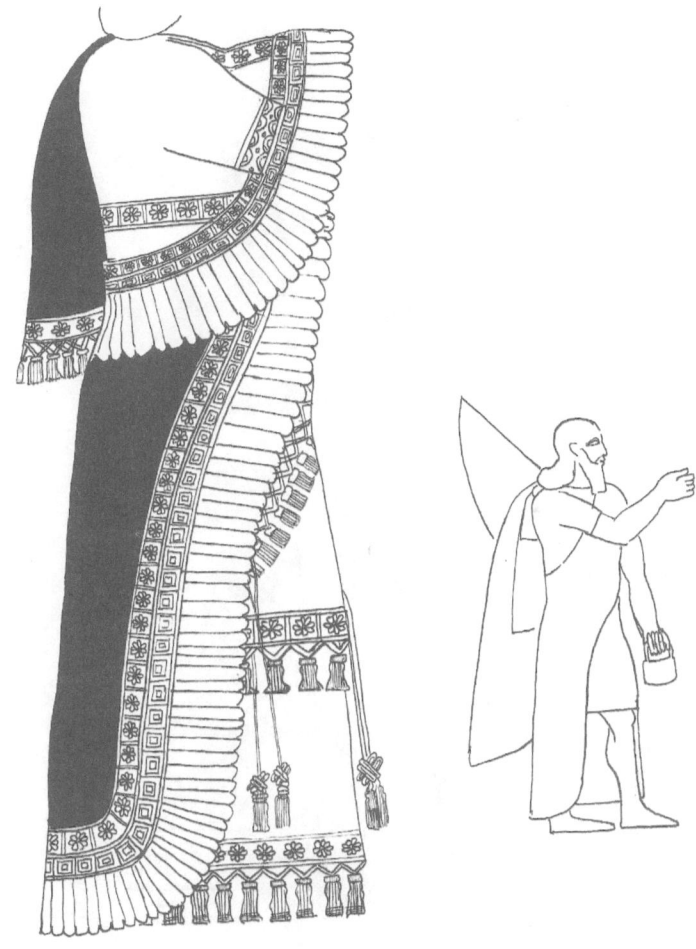

A detailed example of an Assyrian dress and coat similar in design and decoration to the costume of kings.

Layard, A. H. The Monuments of Nineveh, Volume 2, Pl: 34

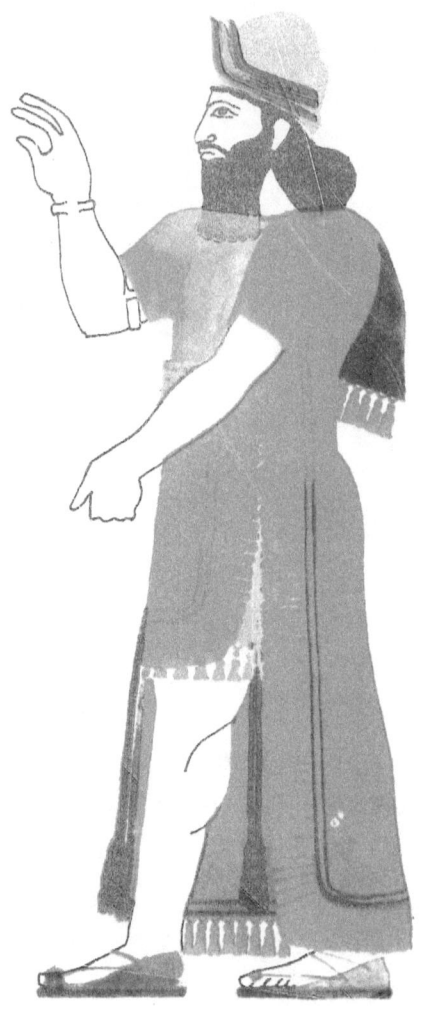

A sketch for a costume of a god wearing a short tunic, covered with a gown around its middle. Then a long dress that is open in the front with fringes similar to those of the gown. On the dress there is the rectangular shawl decorated with similar fringes. There are also some decorating ropes hanging from the margins of the gown. From the palace of king Ashurnasirpal the second (883-859 BC) from the city of Nimrud preserved today in the British Museum.

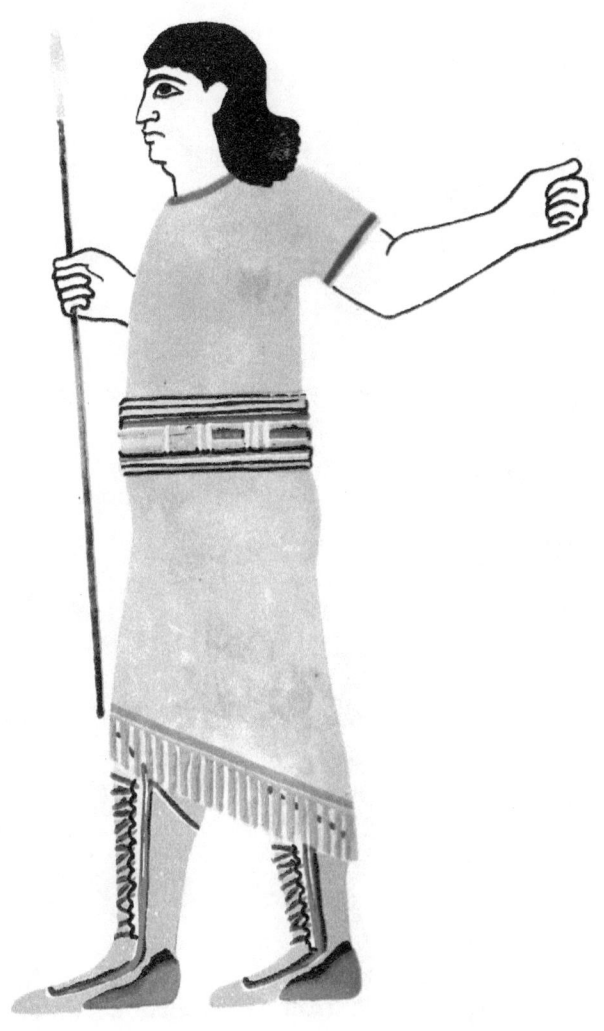

A sketch for King Ashurbanipal's horse wrangler. Note the lower part of the gown, and the boots also used by some ranks of the Assyrian army.

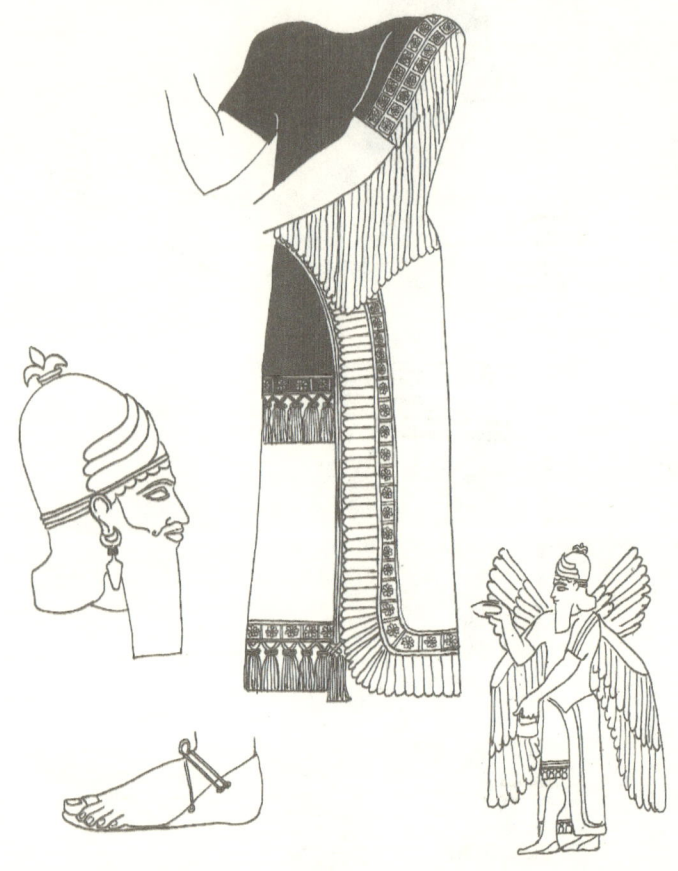

A sketch of a costume taken from a winged persona. The flowers decorating the gown are considered the main decorative unit for costumes. At the same time they were used in architecture, and in Assyrian pottery.

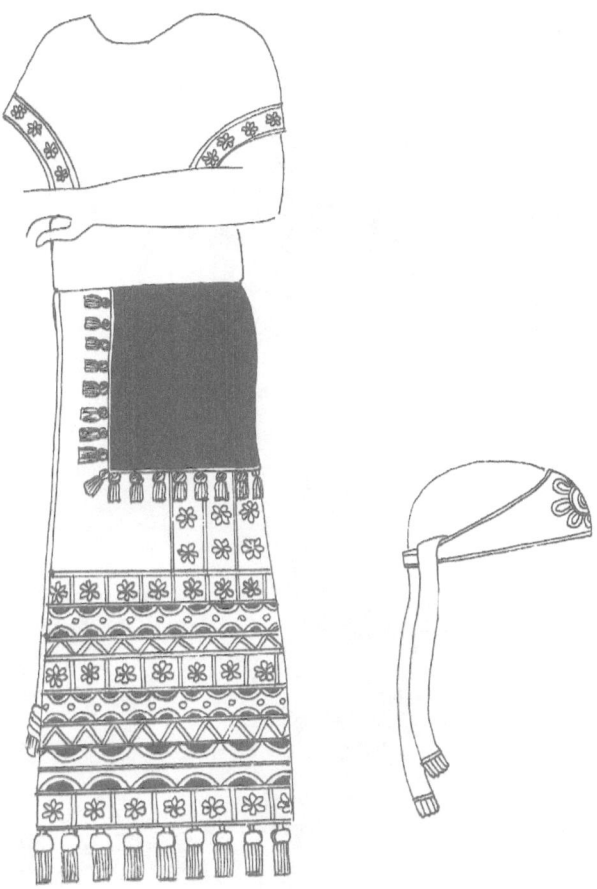

A costume of an Assyrian minister characterized by abundant decorative formations at the lower end, additional piece of cloth tied to the waist using a wide belt. This piece is decorated and had fringes on three edges.

Layard, A.H. Vol. 2, Pl: 23

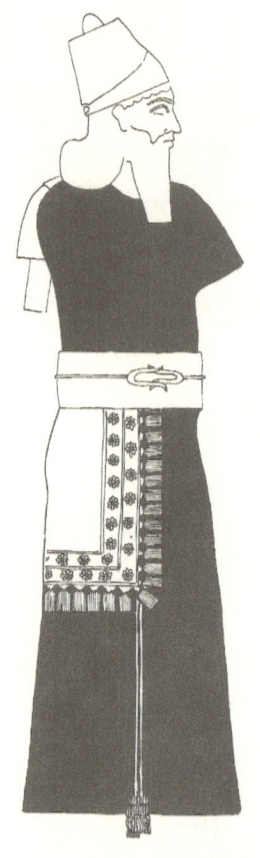

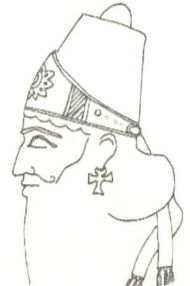

The Assyrian king Ashurnasirpal in a ceremonial costume after returning from a victory for his troops. This is taken from a very large sculpted mural from Nimrud. See a detailed headwear that is not as high as those of the succeeding era. Note the large golden flower that is decorating the front of the crown, which ends by two bands that dangled on the back.

1. **Layard, A.H. Vol. 2, Pl: 32.**
2. **Frankfort, H. The Art and Architecture of the Ancient Orient, Seed. Edit. London 1958.**

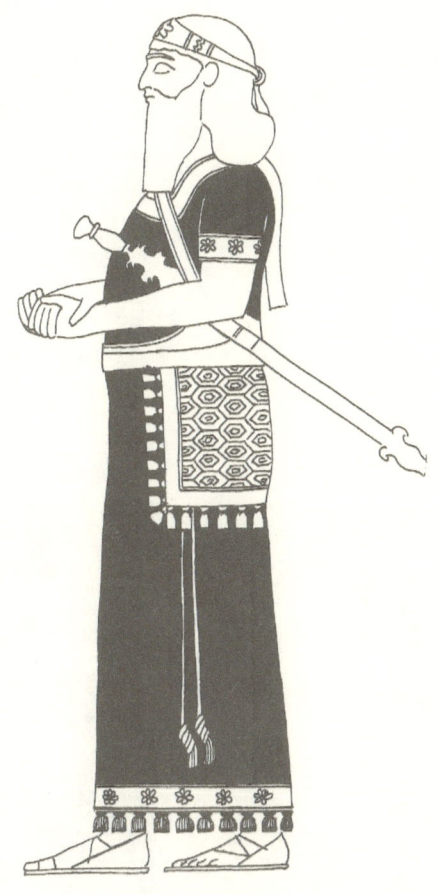

A sketch for the costume of a minister or a retinue of king Ashurnasirpal. See the similarity to the king's costume, limiting the difference to the decorative elements and the headwear. Also see the detailed pattern of the decorated cloth around the waist. The headwear is decorated with the decorative flower that must be smaller than that of the king's crown.

1. **Layard, A.H. Pl: 12.**
2. **Perrot, G. et Ch, Chipiez II fig. 205.**

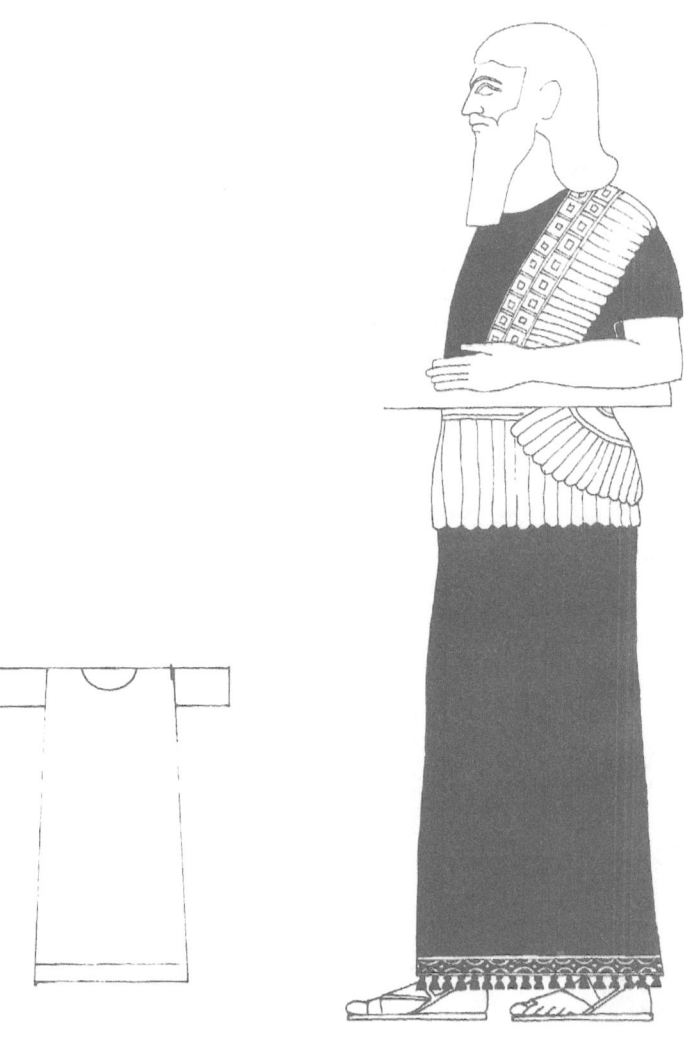

A sketch for an Assyrian musician taken fro a sculpture in Nimrud dating to the era of king Ashurnasirpal. See the paucity of decorative adornments. On the upper body, see the shawl with fringes that is wrapped around the body and covers the right shoulder as well.

M.G. Houston. Ancient Egyptian, Mesopotamian, and Persian Costumes. 2nd Edition, London, 1964.

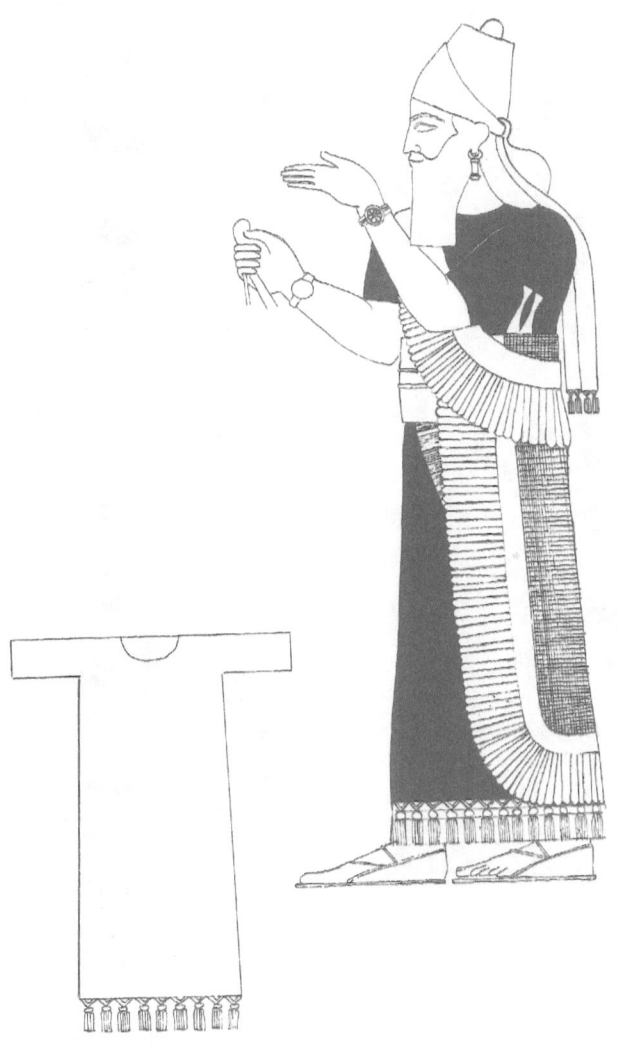

A profile sketch of a costume for king Ashurnasirpal holding a bow in his left hand while he was presenting the sacred sacrifice. The costume was dedicated to religious ceremonies. It is composed of tasseled coat and the main gown decorated with fringes knotted at the upper end.

Perrot, G, etch, Chipiez. Historie de l'art Dans L'Antiquite. Tome II.

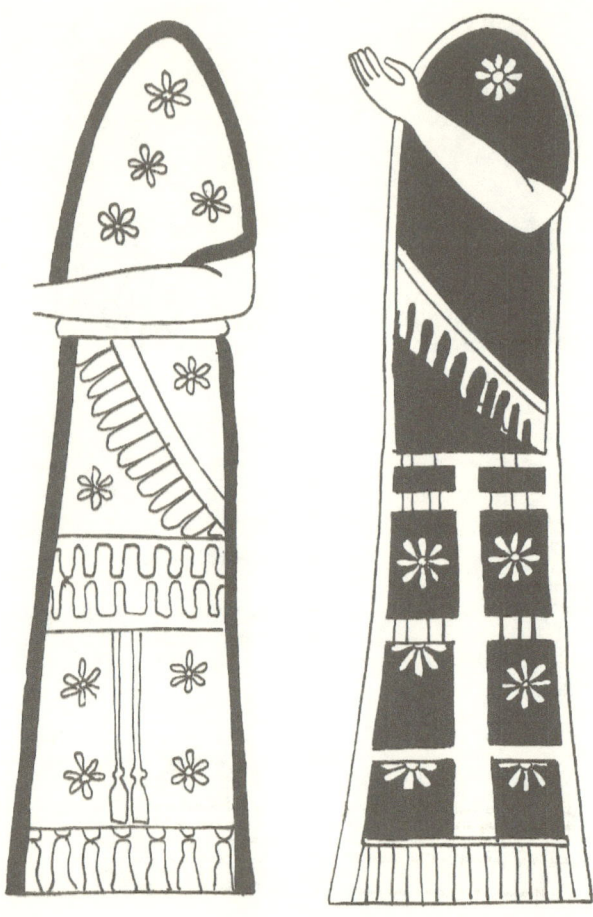

A sketch for King Ashurnasirpal and a retinue behind him. It is taken from a mural built from colorful bricks. See the similarity between decorative elements, which are either large flowers in form of embossed embroidery or gold flowers. See also the distal end of the gown and the different tassels.

George Rawlinson. The Five Great Monarchies of Ancient Eastern World, New York. Vol: II.

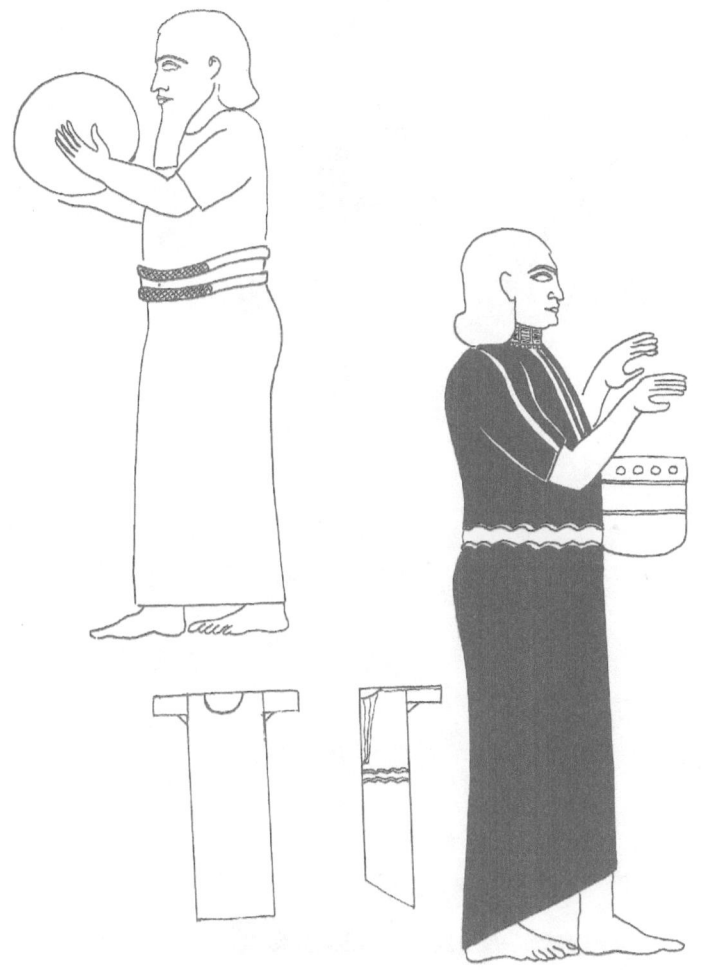

A. A sketch of an Assyrian sculpture representing a musical group in active play, one playing the tambourine. See his simple costume that is devoid of decorations except for the belt around his waist, which is entwined like a rope on the front part.

B. Another Assyrian artist playing the drum. See his costume that is different in many aspects, the head aperture, the belt, and the distal end.

Meissner, Babylonian und Assyrien. Heidelberg 1920. I.P. 334-335.

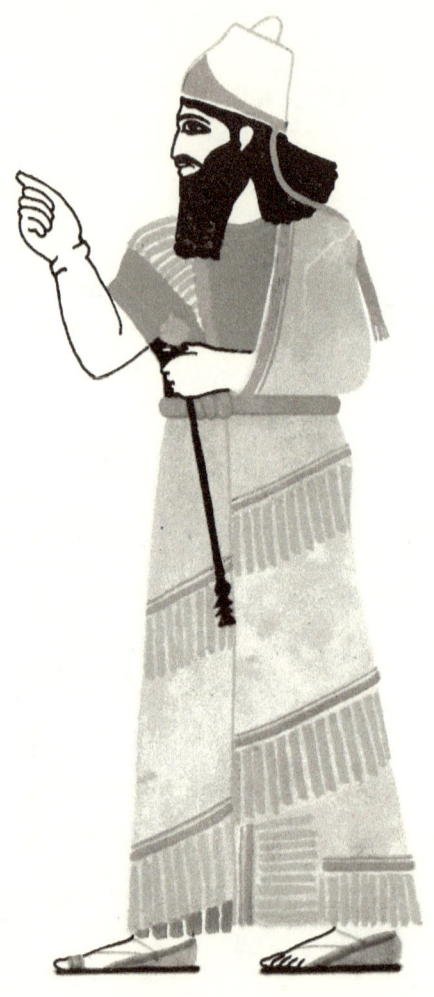

A sketch of an Assyrian king during a religious and ritual ceremony before the sacred tree (the tree of life). See the coat wrapped around the long gown with fringes. The king is holding his royal staff.

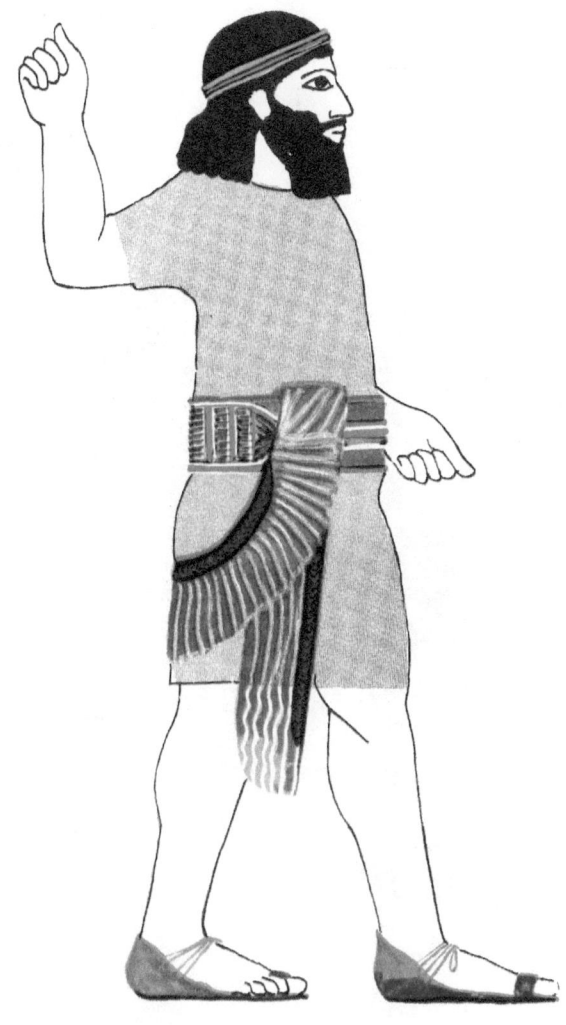

A sketch for a horse wrangler in the Assyrian army. See a different gown and the way of wrapping, also the head band and the sandals.

E. Strommenger. The Art of Mesopotamia. London. 1964. Fig: 191; 260; 231.

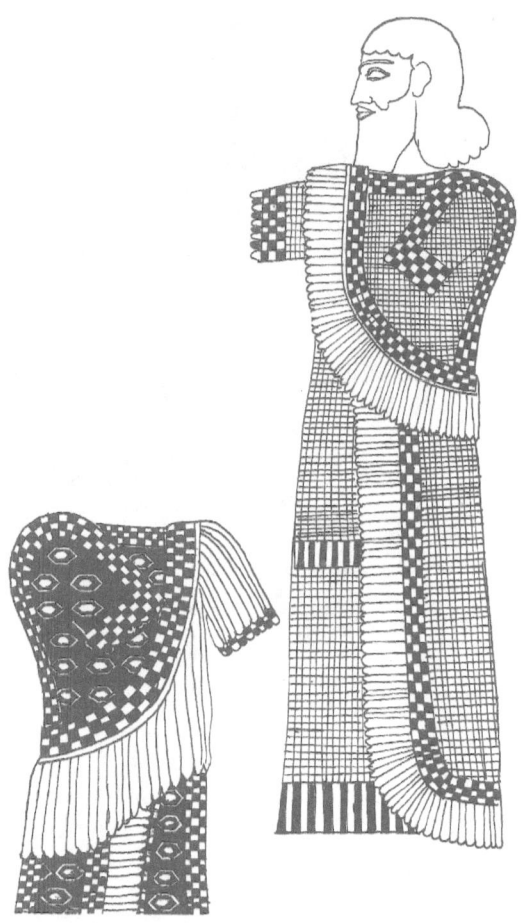

A. A sketch of mural colorful drawings from the Assyrian territory Til Barsib (Red Hill) from the 8th century BC. The sketch represents two Assyrians in colorful costumes, red, blue, and red-brown. Here is an Assyrian coat decorated with squares in red and light blue. The lateral and the inferior tassels are colored in blue.

B. A sketch for a costume of a winged mythical persona from the same location with same colors. The upper outer edges and the coat decorated with different decorative formations.

A. Parrot. Assur. Paris 1961 Fig: 109, 110.

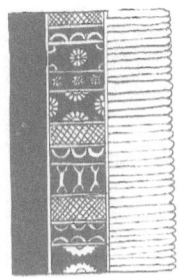
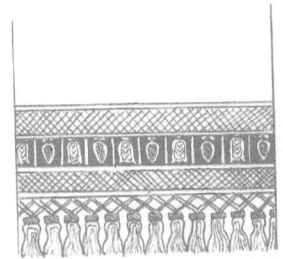

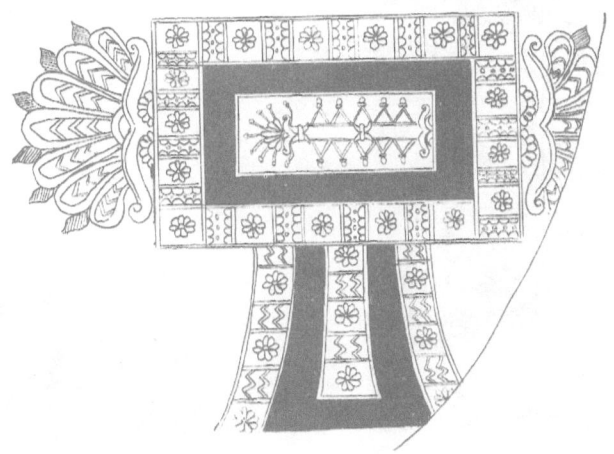

A & B: Two sketches of decorations in from of tassels in different decorative elements bordered from the top by parallel formations of popular subjects among the Assyrians. These samples were commonly used at the distal ends of the royal and gods costumes.

C. Embroidery of plant formations and additional decorative elements such as the sacred tree. This formation reflects embroidered decorations on the upper segment of the gown for a winged mythical persona.

    1. **Layard, H. I.pl. 51.**

    2. **Perrot G. et ch, chipiez. Hist. De l'ant,. II fig: 445.**

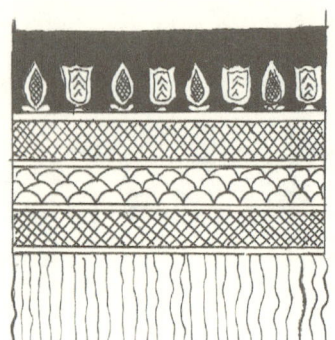

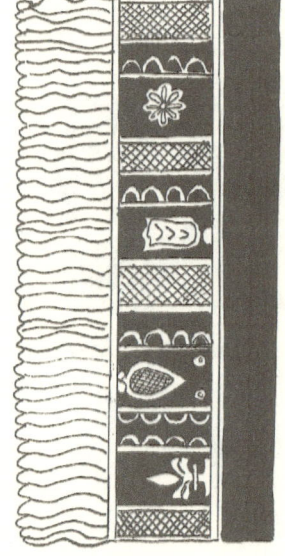

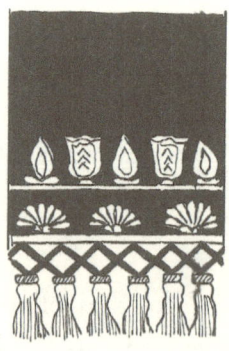

Sketches of additional decorations used on the distal ends of gowns
and coats used on some Assyrian winged persona.
Layard, H. I .Pl.35, 36.

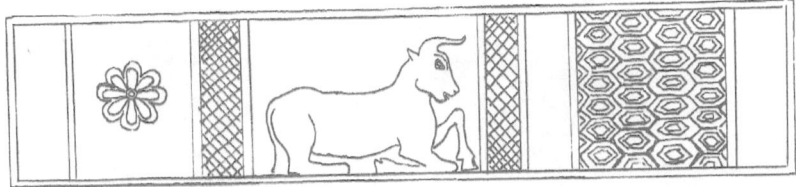

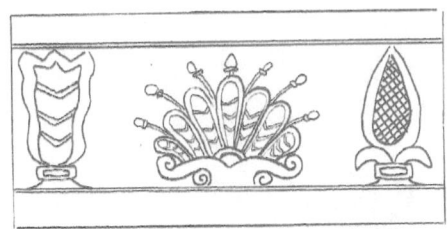

Sketches of diverse embroidered formations used mostly for decorating the front and upper parts of the Assyrian gowns reflecting diverse subjects such as animals, and plants.

Layard, H. I. pis 34, 48

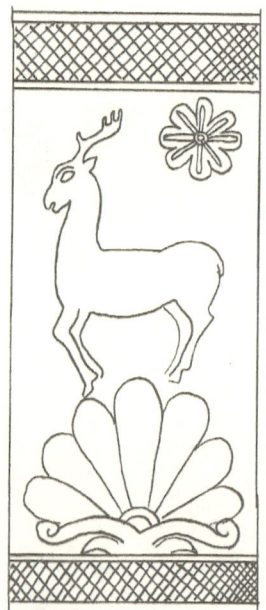

Sketches of other examples of animals, and birds embroidered on Assyrian costumes.

Layard, H. I. pls 34, 48.

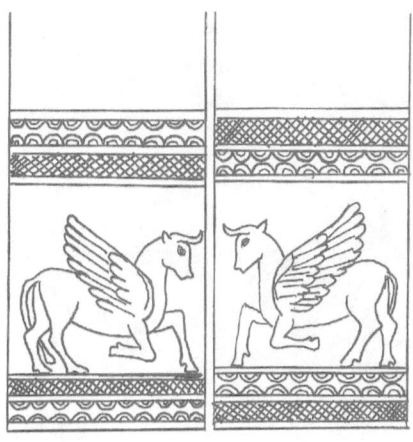

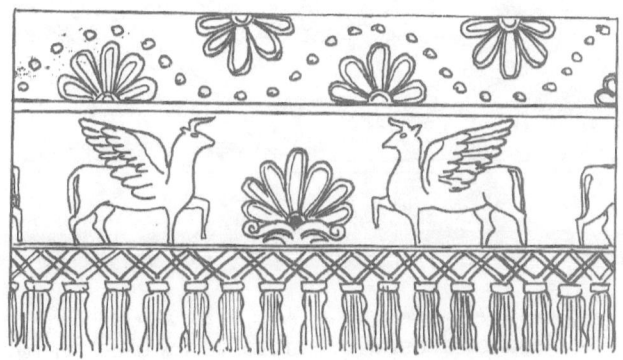

Sketches of embroidered decorations used on upper parts of Assyrian royal costumes.
Layard, H. pl: 36, 46.

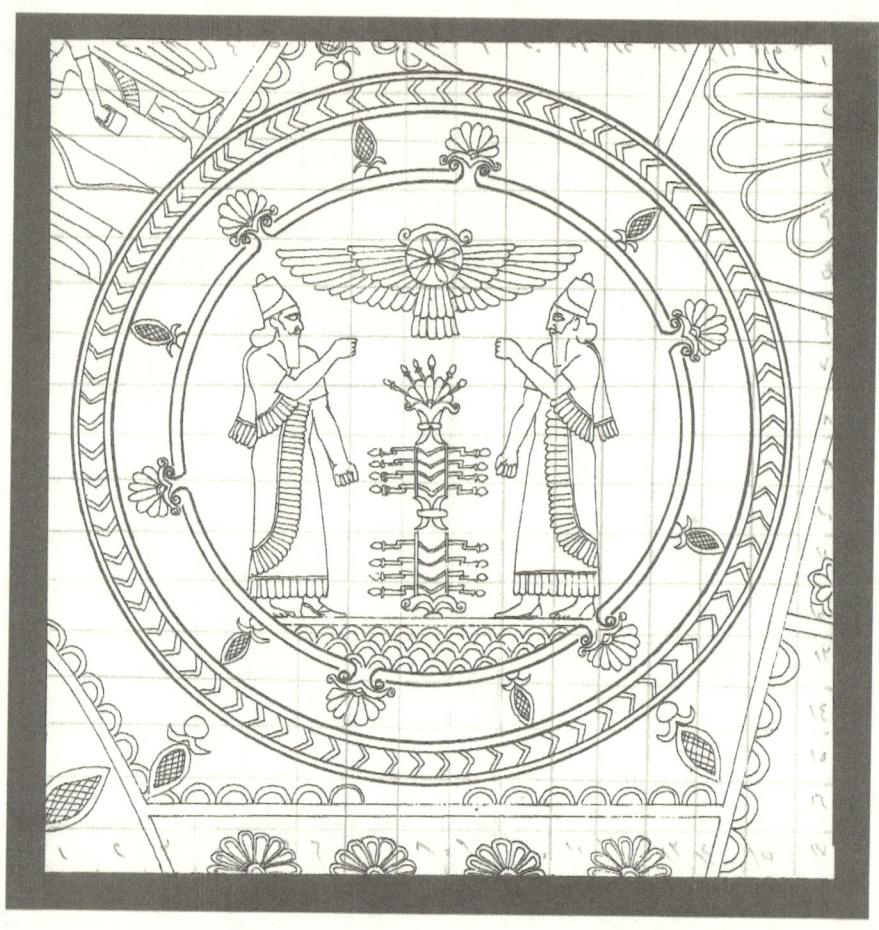

A sketch of subjects of decorative embroideries used for royal costume on the front aspect of the chest.

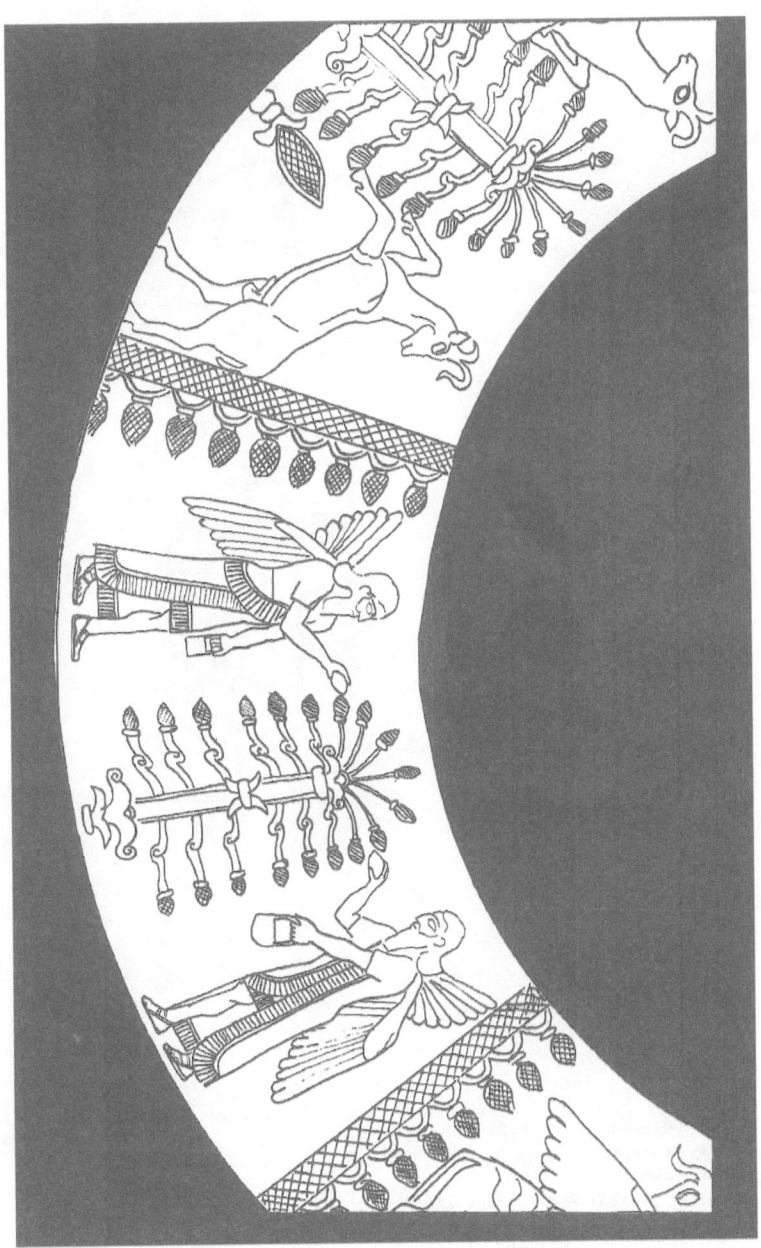

Sketch of decorative embroideries on royal costumes on the front aspect of the chest. Note the sacred tree surrounded by winged gods in the form of humans, and a similar formation with animals surrounding the sacred tree.

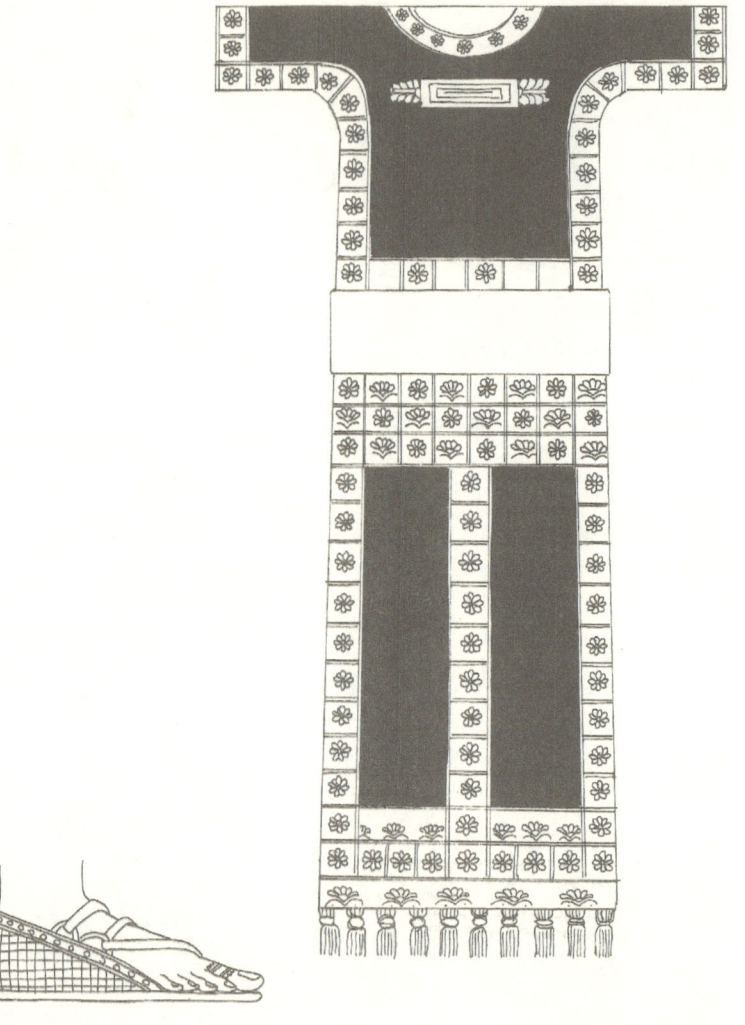

A. A different style of decorative formations in royal Assyrian costumes. Note the absence of a coat.

    1. Layard, H. I. pl. 18.

    2. Babelon E. Manuel d'Archeologie orientale. Paris 1888.

B. A sketch for a sample of royal shoes in form of a leather sandal with some metal rings through which leather bands are used to secure the sandal in place. Note the ring around the large toe.

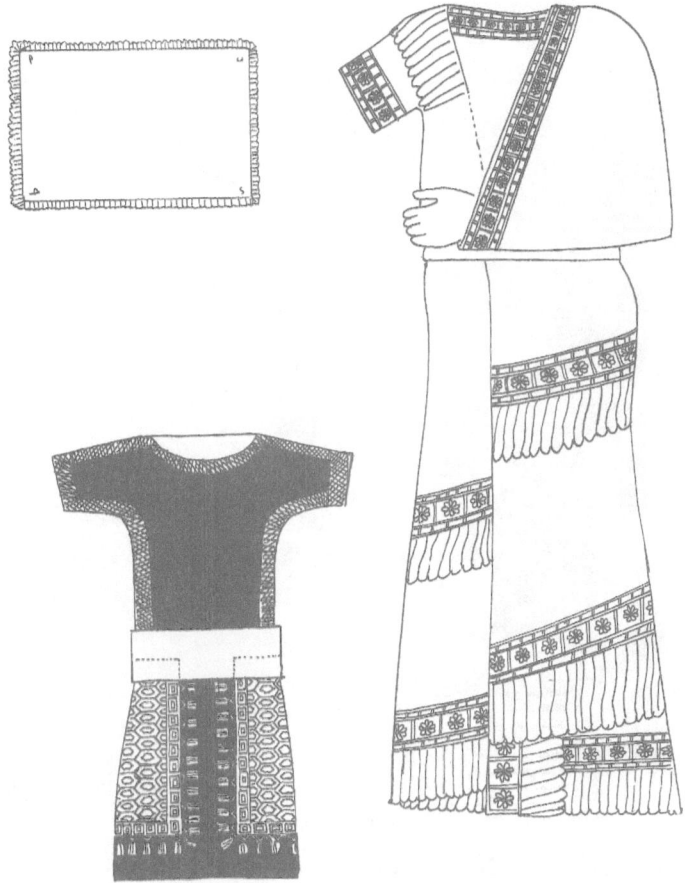

A. A sketch of a royal official costumes during ritual and religious ceremony in front the sacred tree. The tunic is poorly defined but is covered with a gown all the way down to the feet. There is what simulates a shawl through which the king pushed his hand carrying the royal staff.

B. A sketch for an Assyrian king in hunting outfit. Note the intricate embroidery at the margins of the outfit. Also note the tasseled piece surrounding his waist, which is held in place with a wide belt.

Layard, H. I.pl.25, 51, 18.

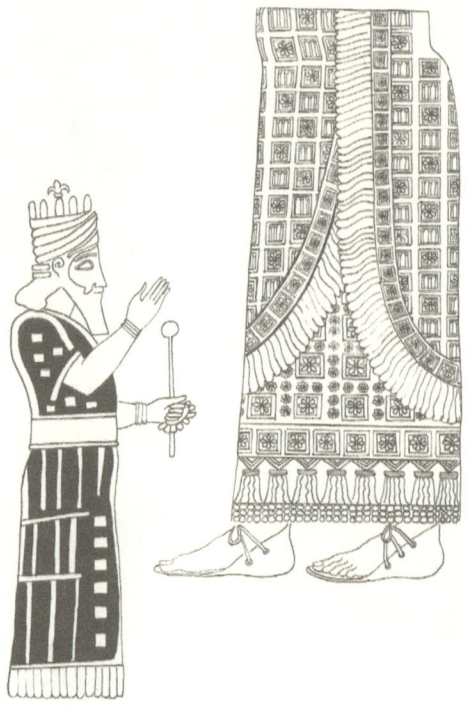

A. A sketch of a distal part of a royal costume, which is composed of long tunic covered with a gown that is open on the front but held together by tassels. Note the diverse shape and sizes of the gold pieces used for decoration. Note the squared decorative formations with golden flowers or longitudinal and transverse lines within.

B. A sketch for god Ashur from a drawing in colors over glass wall taken from the city of Ashur, a rare example of colored Assyrian ruins. The decorations are not so different from the royal ones, except for the headwear, where the gods have multiple pair of horns, a symbol for divinity. God Ashur is standing on a platform holding his famous staff.

    1. **Botta. P.E. et Falndin. E. Monument de Ninvie tome II. Paris. 1849-1850 pl.101.**

    2. **W. Andrae. Assur, Farbige Keramik, Berlin, 1923, p.10.0.**

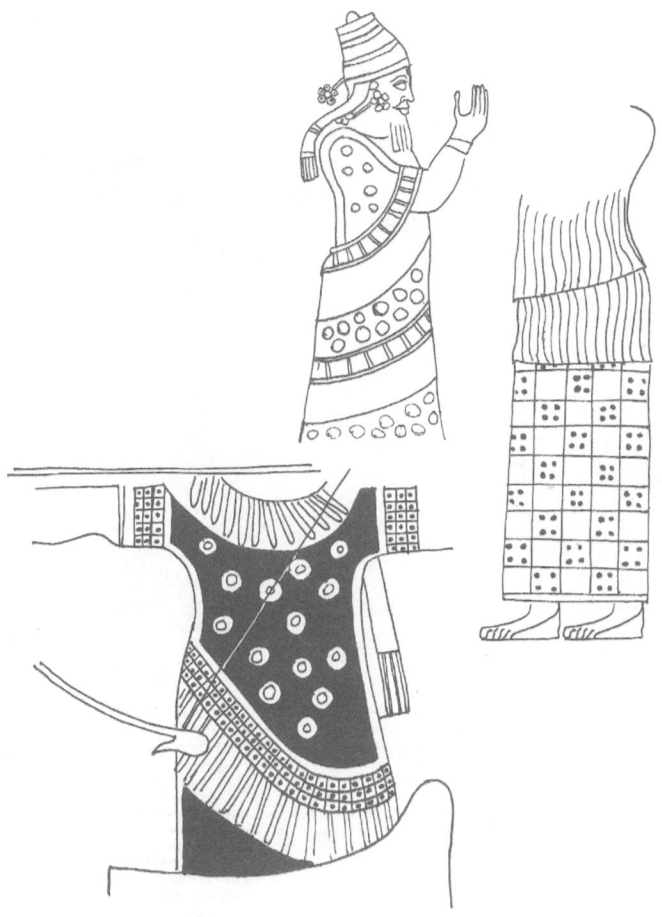

A & B: A sketch of other Assyrian royal costumes in different
   decorations. One has small gold circles attached for decoration
   while the second one has larger gold pieces sewn to the coat.

C: The upper end of a royal hunting outfit.

Oppenheim, L. Journal of Near Eastern Studies VIII 1948.

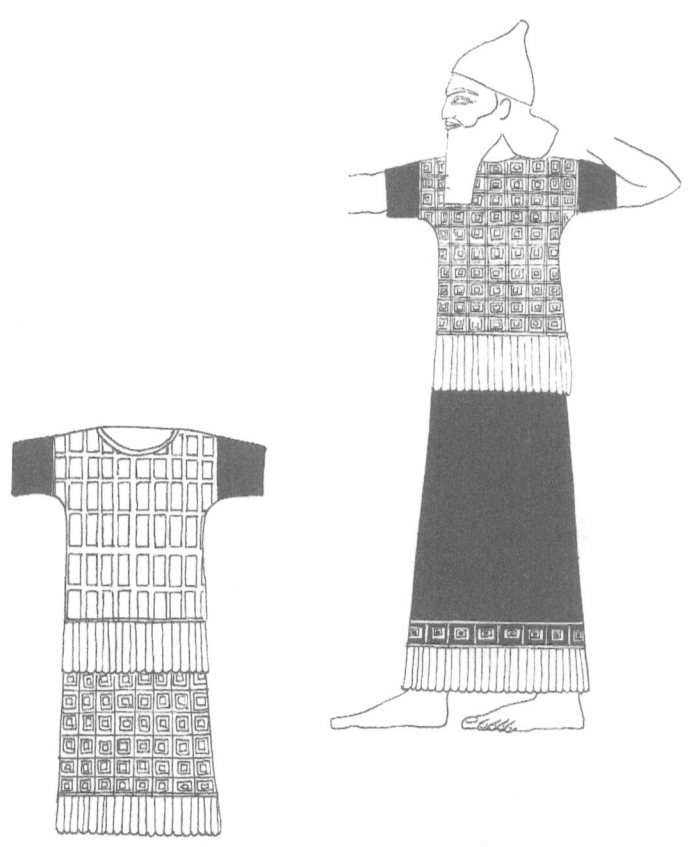

A. A sketch from an Assyrian mural in Nimrud taken from a scene of Assyrian siege to Israel. The sketch depicts the royal war costume of Assyrian king Tiglat-Pileser the third (744-727 BC). Note the tasseled, short-sleeved and non-decorated tunic, over which a tasseled armored vest made of leather is usually worn.

B. A sketch from the same mural, depicting the defeat of the enemy and the speed at which the Assyrian Calvary overtake them. The sketch depicts the outfit of an Assyrian caval similar in general to the previous warrior except in decorations. The upper part is usually made of leather.

Sidney Smith. Assyrian Sculptues in the British Museum. London, 1938.

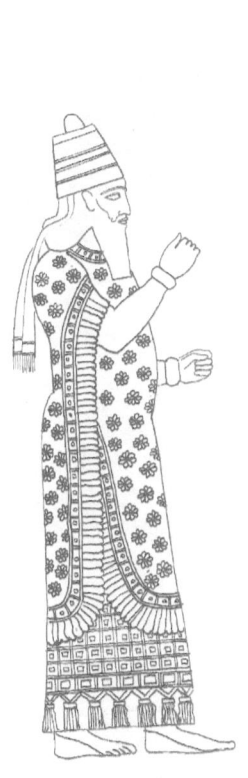
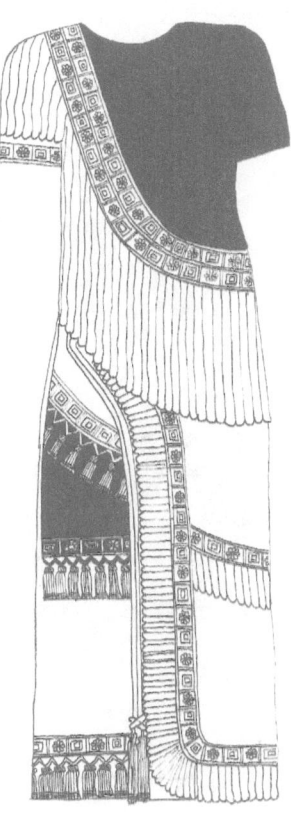

A. Sketch for a costume of king Sargon the second with its intricate decorative details. It is taken from a sculpture found in Khorsabad, and is preserved today in the Louvre museum in Paris.

B. A sketch for a costume of King Sennacherib revealing the intricate embroidery and adornments. The coat is decorated with adornments and golden flowers.

    1. Parrot A. Assur.

    2. Max Kellner. The Assyrian Monuments, Boston 1900.

    3. Parrot, A. Niniveh et l'ancien testament. Paris 1955 fig. 12.

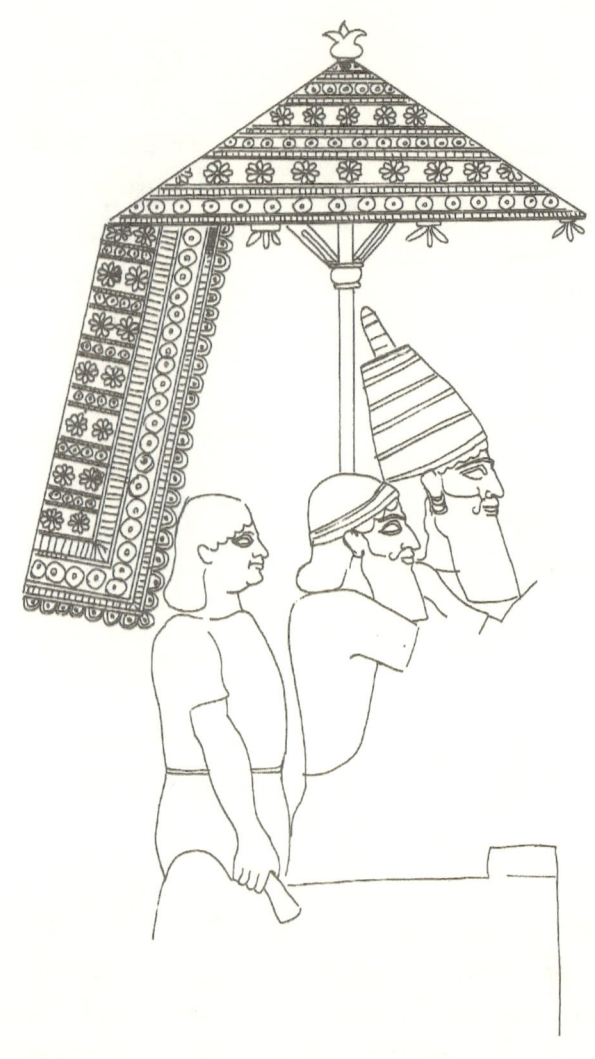

A sketch of a royal carriage and umbrella with decorations simulating
what is seen on the royal costumes.
Perrot G et ch. Chipiez de l'art II, 211.

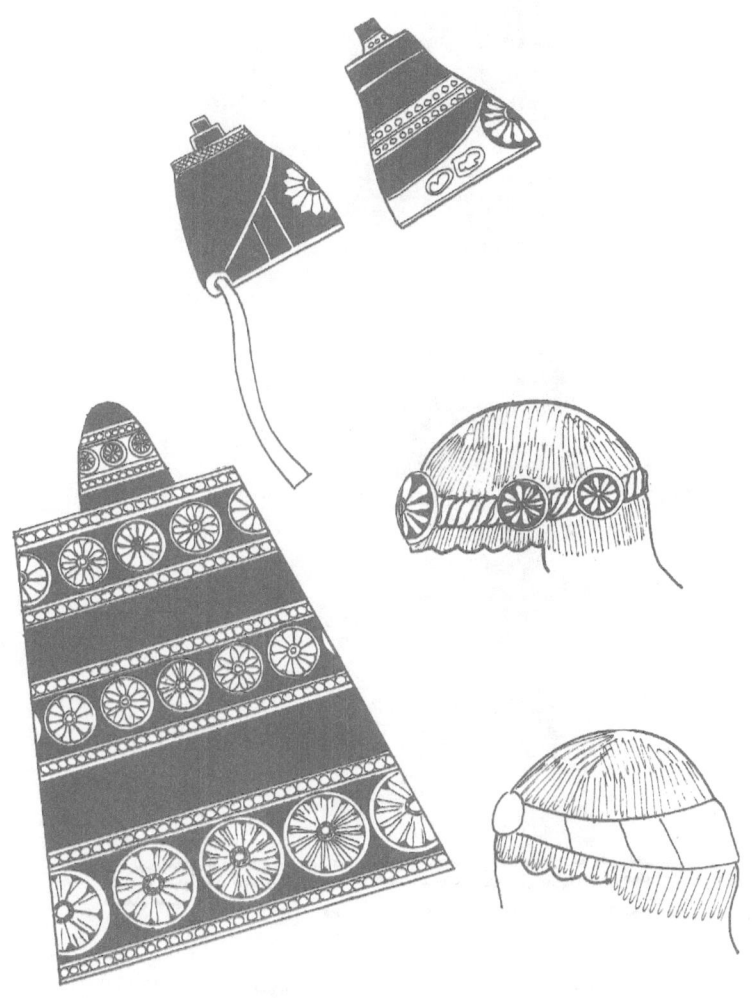

A sketch of different headwear for the learned Assyrian king
Ashurbanipal. Note the tiers decorated with jewelry. It is known that
Assyrian kings used different headwear according to the occasion, those
specific to religious ceremonies, hunting, or war.

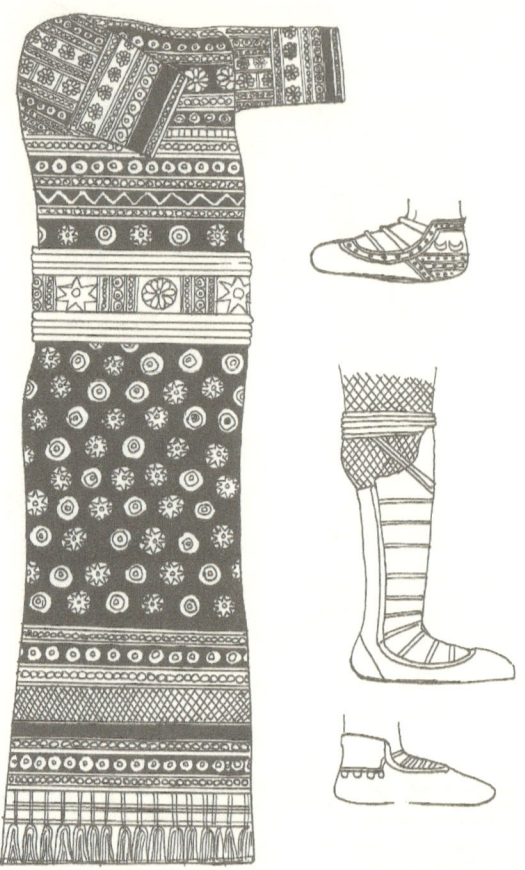

A sketch for a ceremonial costume of King Ashurbanipal reflecting diverse decorative elements. Note the shoes, including the hunting shoes that are different from its counterpart from the primordial era of King Sargon.

G.R. Mayer. Altorientalische Denkmaler Im Vorderasiatischen Museum Berlin-Leipzig 1965.

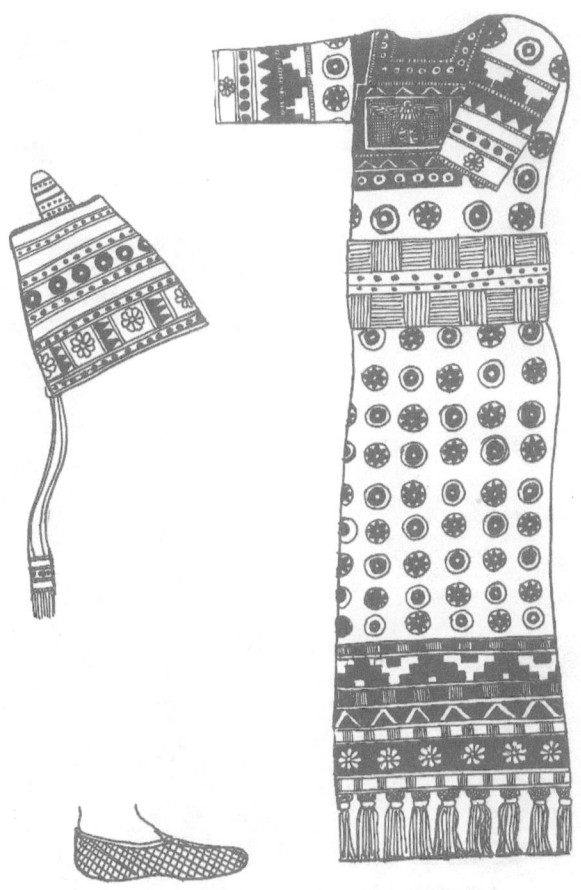

A sketch for King Ahurbanipal's hunting outfit copied from sculptures in the British Museum simulating the costumes of King Marduk-nadin-ahhe (1050 BC) decorated at the upper part with the Assyrian symbol; the winged disc with the sacred tree beneath, and the headwear of this king.

1. **Gadd, C.J. The Assyrian Sculpture. London 1934.**
2. **Houston, M.G. Fig. 148.**

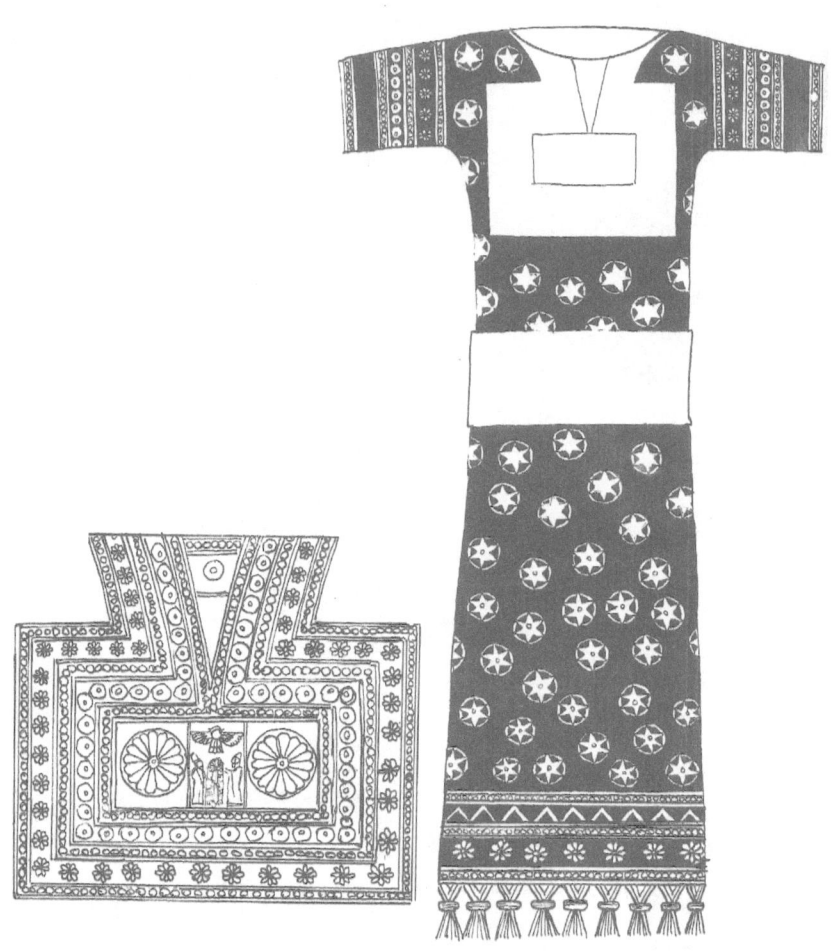

A sketch of a costume for King Ashurbanipal taken from a sculpture dating to the same era. The costume is decorated with diverse decorations particularly in the upper part where two large flowers surround a piece containing two humans, each on one side of the sacred tree and the Assyrian symbol above.

Strommenger, E. The Art of Mesopotamia. London 1964.

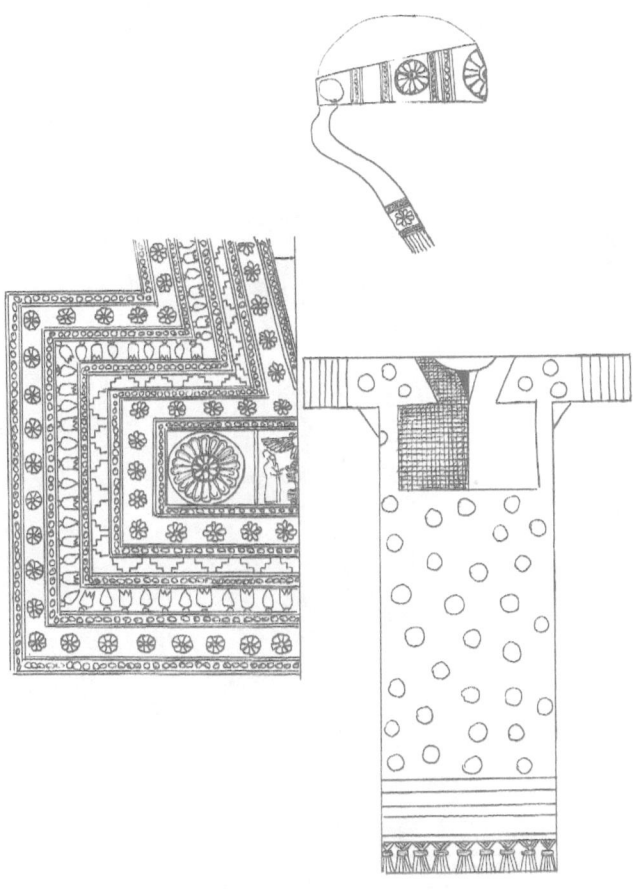

A sketch for another costume for King Ashurbanipal with a sketch for his headwear. The headwear is in form of a wide band decorated in front with gold flower, and a band decorated at its tails.
Strommenger, E. The Art of Mesopotamia. London 1964.

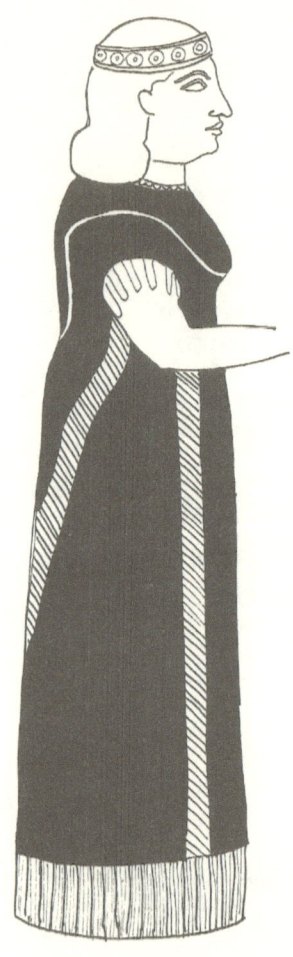

A sketch of an Assyrian woman costume dating to the late Assyrian era taken from a clay vessel found in Ashur city.

Walter Andrae, Colored Ceramics from Ashur, London 1925 Fig. 30, 32.

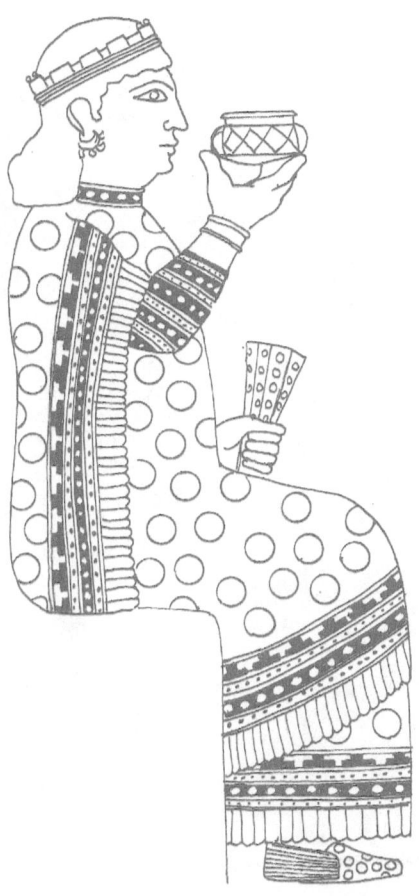

A sketch of a rare costume for an Assyrian woman, found on a sculpture in Nineveh, depicting king ashurbanipal's wife, Ashursharrat.

Hall, H.R. Babylonian and Assyrian Sculpture in British Museum Paris, 1928 pl. XLI.

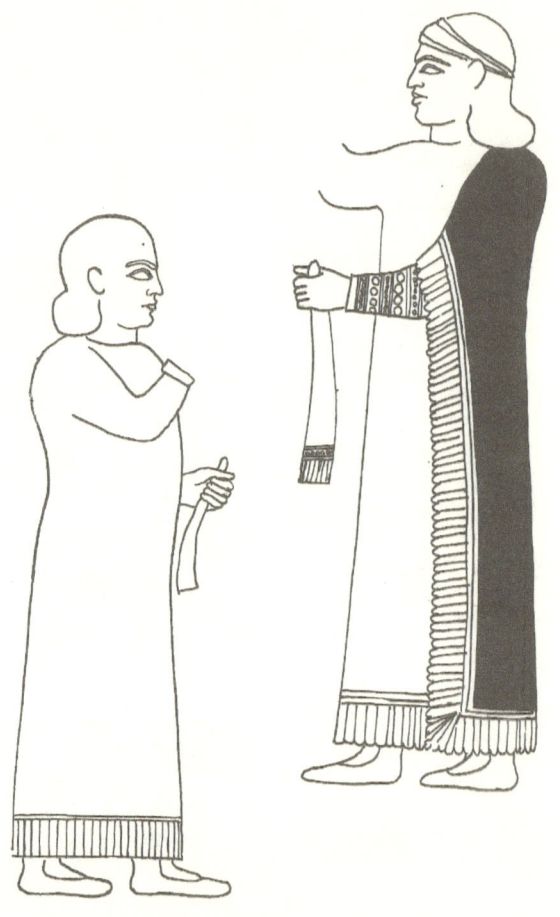

A sketch of female costume of King Ashurbanipal's retinues depicting the differences compared to the costume of Queen Ashrsharrat.

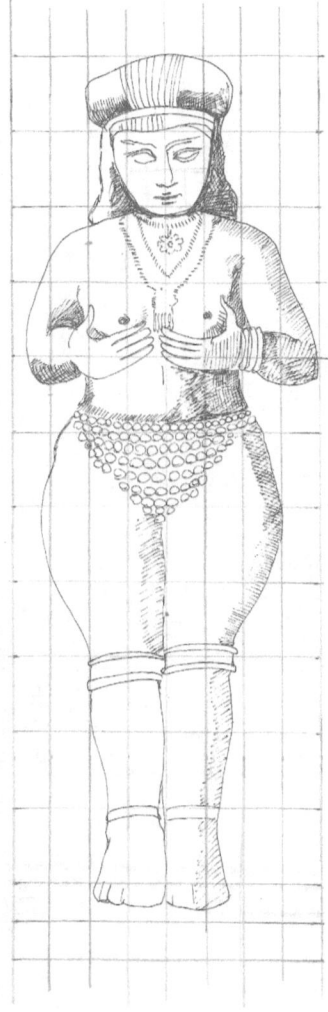

A sketch of Ishtar, the sensual goddess of love and war among Semitic people, also known as goddess Innana among Sumerians.

Hall, H.R. Babylonian and Assyrian Sculpture in British Museum Paris, 1928 pl. XLI.

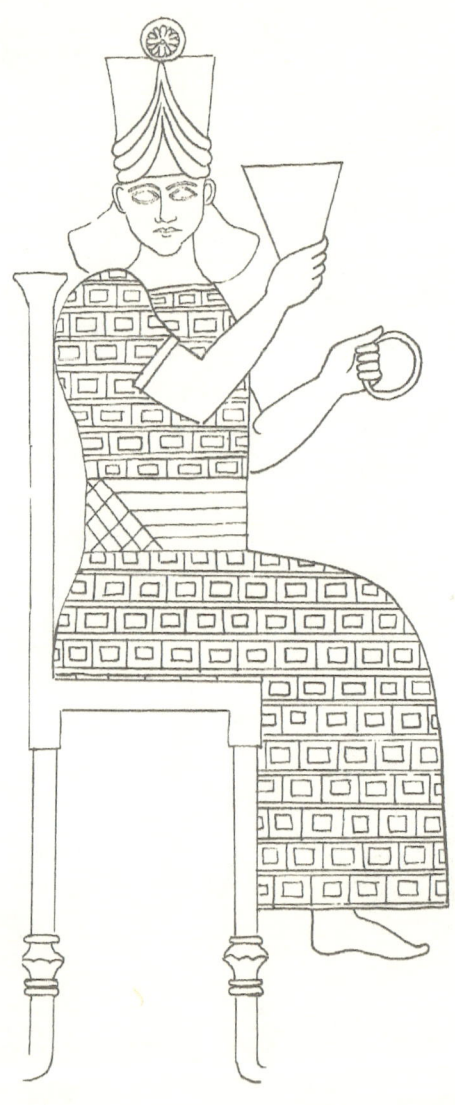

A sketch of another female costume taken from a religious ceremony representing the transfer of gods by soldiers. It is known that when the Assyrians raided the Babylonians and in revenge, transferred god Marduk to the their kingdom as a pillage.

Layard, H. Monuments. Pl.65.

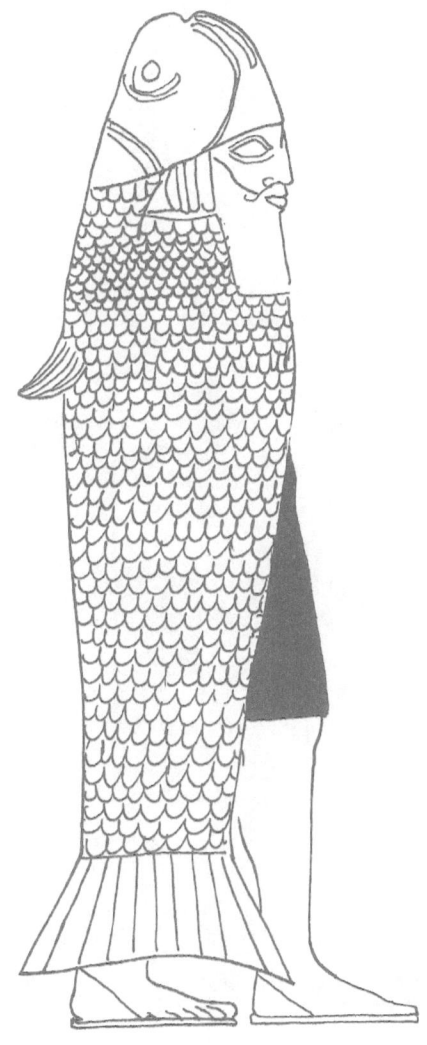

A sketch of ceremonial costumes worn by clergymen during ritual ceremony. It is composed of a tunic down to the level of the knees, usually made of white linen, covered with a shell simulating a fish, which holds important ritual symbols (the human- the clergy- the fish)
Perrot G et ch, chipiez. Hist, de L'art II fig. 162.

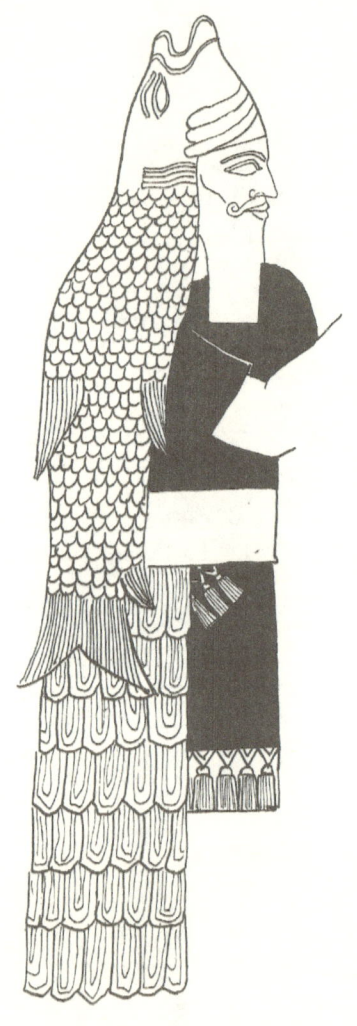

A sketch of god-fish taken from a sculpture found in Nimrud. The costume is composed a short tasseled tunic, wrapped at the middle with another gown covered with a piece covered with decorations similar to fish shells. The head and shoulders are covered with a fish like cover.
Layard, H. II pl. 6.

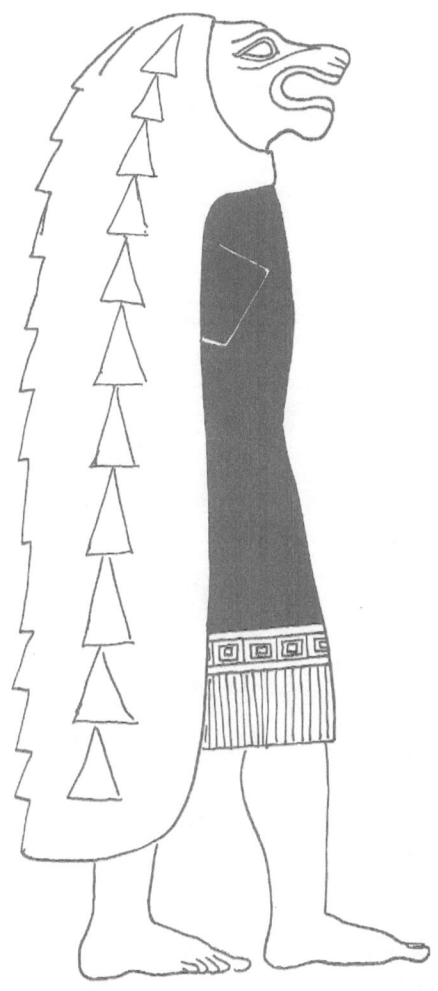

A sketch for another ceremonial costume composed of a tunic with scarce decorations and an animal mask (lion). The objective of such persona (clergymen- men) is to fend evil souls out of the sick.

1. **Frankfort, H. Art and Architecture of the Ancient Orient, London, second edit. 1958**
2. **Perrot, G ch. Chipiez. Hist. De L'art II. Fig. 162.**

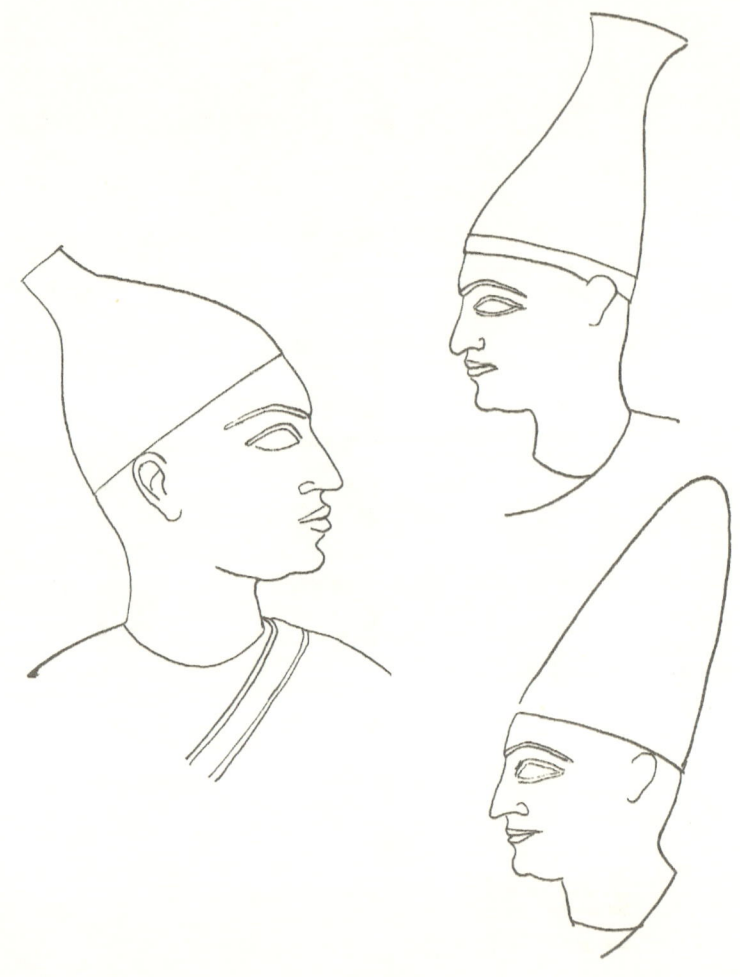

A sketch for different types of headwear, used by clergymen, usually made of linen that was popular among many contemporary civilizations.

B, Meissner, Babylonien und Assyrien Heidelberg 1920-1925.

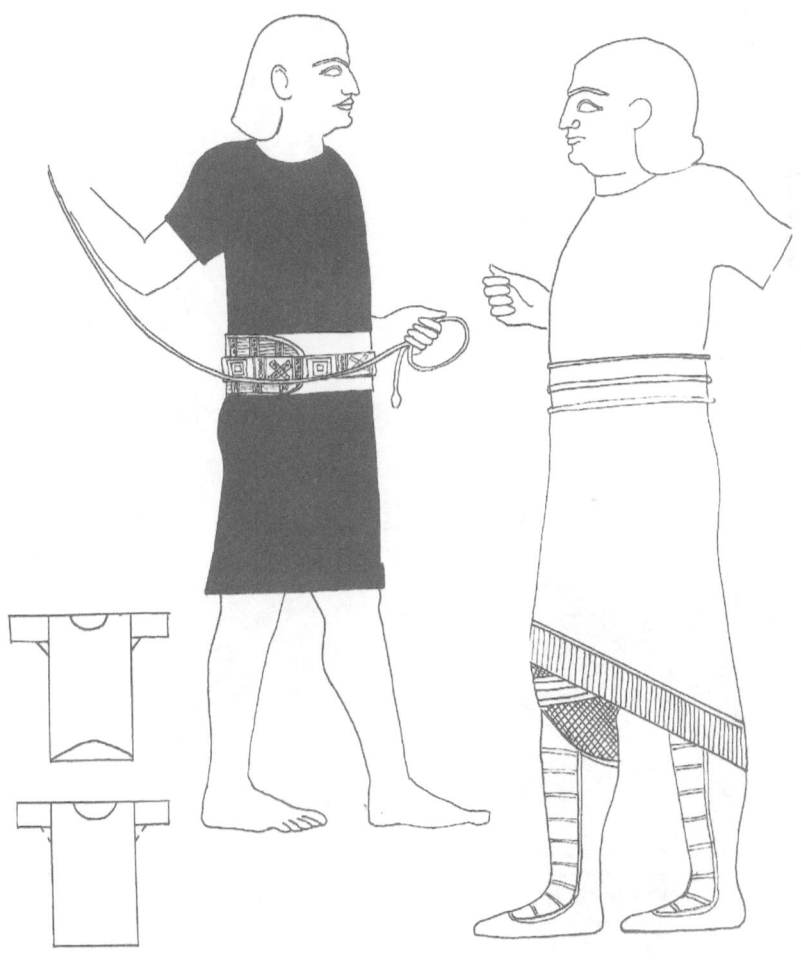

A. A sketch form a mural in Nineveh depicting a donkey wrangler preserved at the British Museum. Note the simple dress devoid of any decorations except the belt.

B. A sketch of an Assyrian horse wrangler. Note the short anterior end to facilitate riding the horse. Also the unique belt looking like three ropes tied to his waist.

Hall, H.R. Babylonian and Assyrian Sculpture pl. LIV.

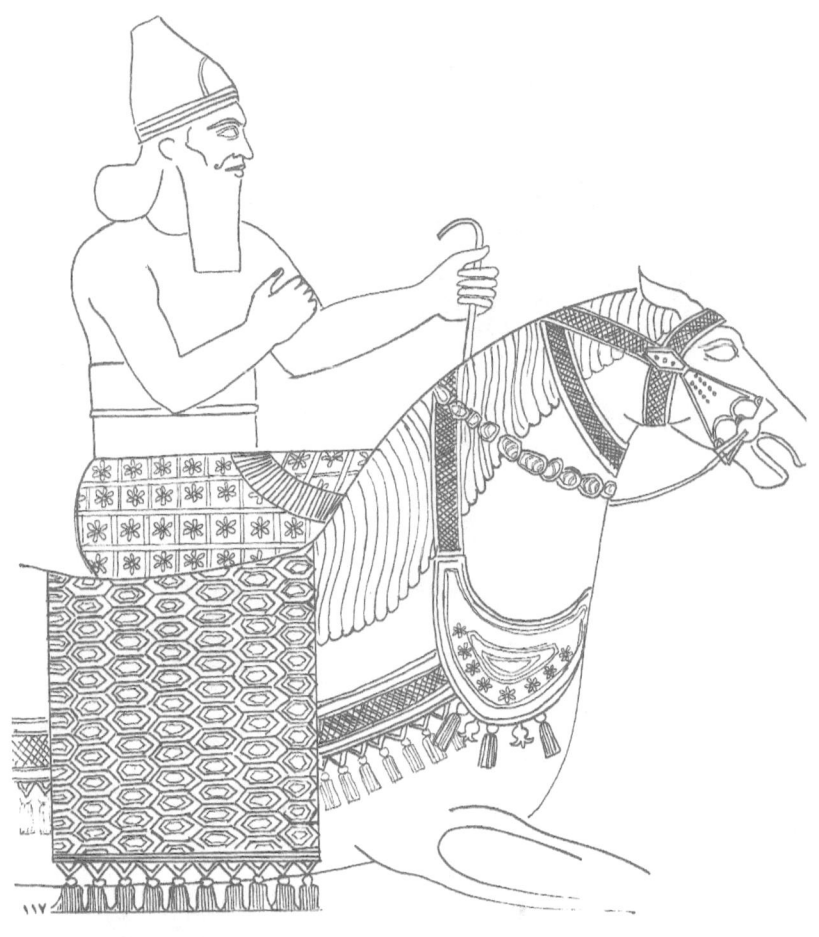

A sketch of an Assyrian warrior in full military gears. Note the loincloth decorated with jewelry in form of small flowers. Also the horse saddle with its decorative adornment including a cloth with fringes simulating a small rug. The compatibility between the decorations and their elements add an atmosphere of artistic harmony so well recognized in many Assyrian decorative subjects.

Layard, H. Monuments II pl. 42.

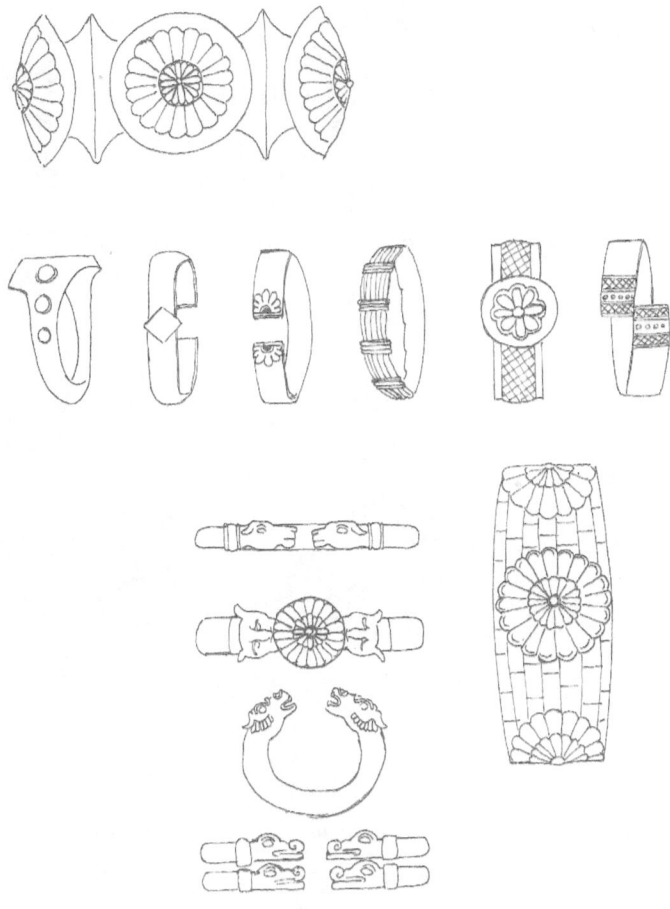

A sketch of different Assyrian bracelets, which were used by high class and the socially affluent Assyrians. Some bracelets were decorated in a similar way to the costumes and were usually seen at the end of the sleeves. Some bracelets ended with heads of mythical animals.

1. **Perrot, G. et ch. Chipiez.**
2. **Layard, H. Monuments. P. 35, 12, 25, 36**
3. **Houston, M.G.**

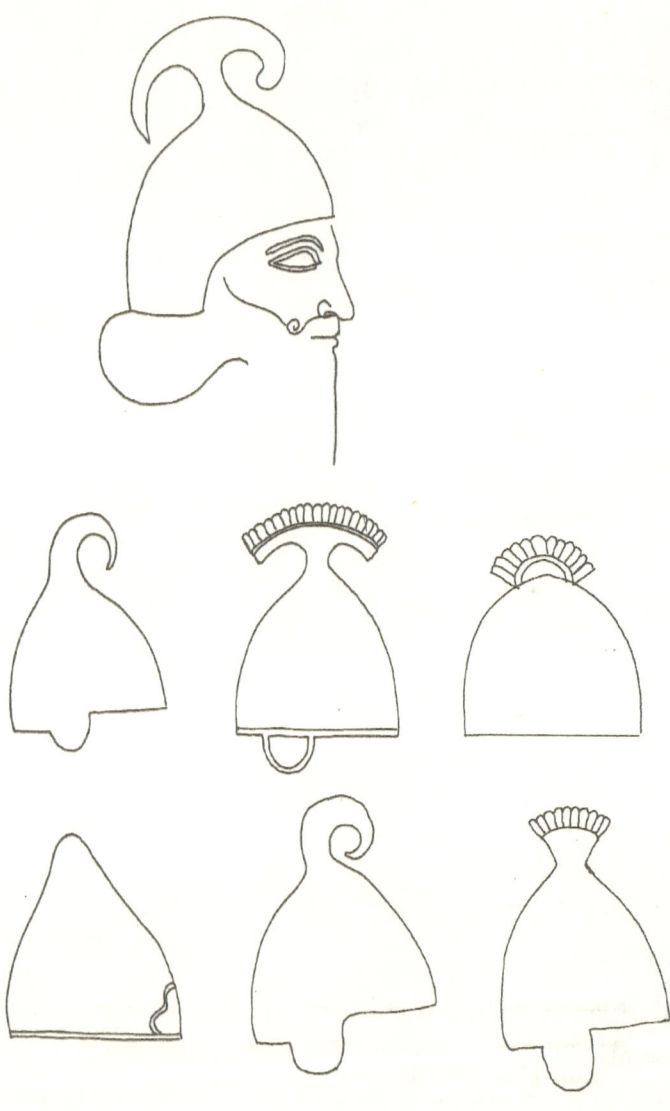

A sketch of different metal helmets used by the Assyrian military, which are similar to the helmets subsequently used by the Greek, some of which are preserved in the British museum. Other types of headwear were made of cloth and or leather.

Layard, H. Monuments pl. 78, 79, 80, 81.

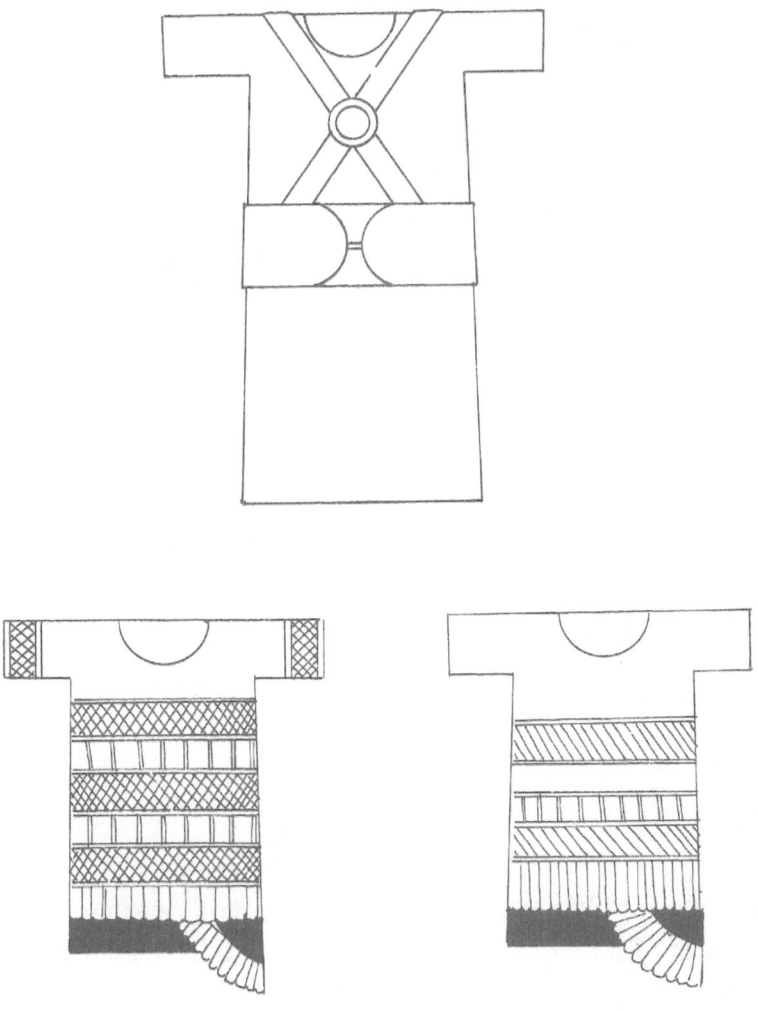

A sketch of Assyrian military outfits. The upper one belongs to a high ranking Cavalry and is usually tied with a belt at the waist. The lower two, represent outfit of soldiers, in which the belt is replaced by a strap decorated with flowers.

Layard, H. Monuments I 26.

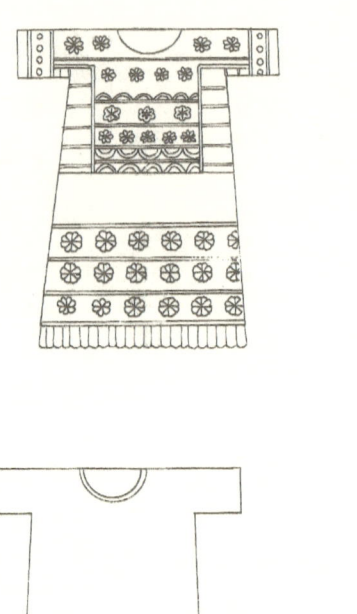
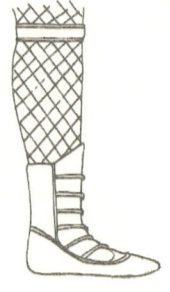
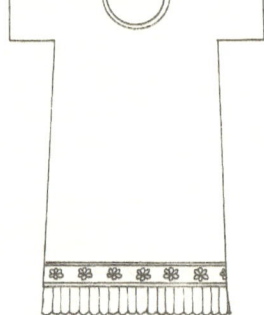

A sketch of gears used by high ranking Assyrian officers;

A. An outfit of an Assyrian Calvary. Note the middle section devoid of decorations.

B. Another military outfit with decorations at the distal end only.

C. A leather boot usually worn over elegant soaks made of cloth or wool. Note the unique design of the soaks where a thin leather band is usually used to secure the soaks in place.

Layard, H. Monuments, I. 26, 16.

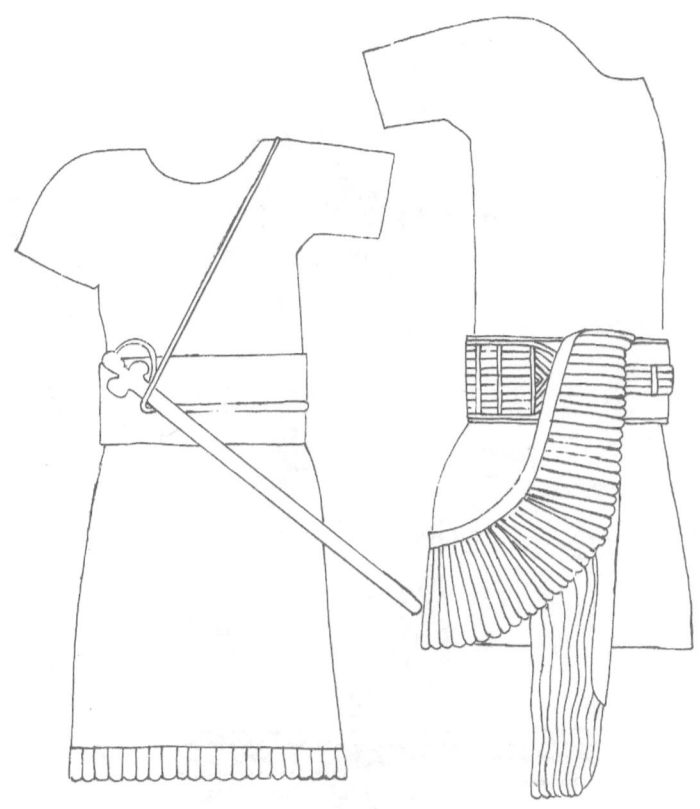

A sketch of other forms of military outfits used by high ranking Assyrian military. Note the differences in their decorations. The vast majority were tied to the body by belts, which also came in different styles. They were much simpler than those used by the kings and gods.

Layard, H. Monuments. I. pl. 22.

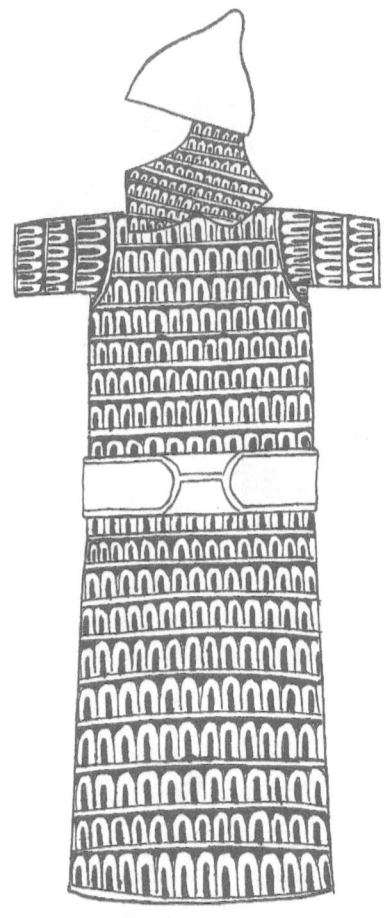

A sketch of an Assyrian warrior in armored outfit most probably made of thick wool and covered with metals. A separate piece is used for the neck that also covers the ears and parts of the face. The helmet is made of metal. The belt can be either made of leather or metal.

Houston, M.G.

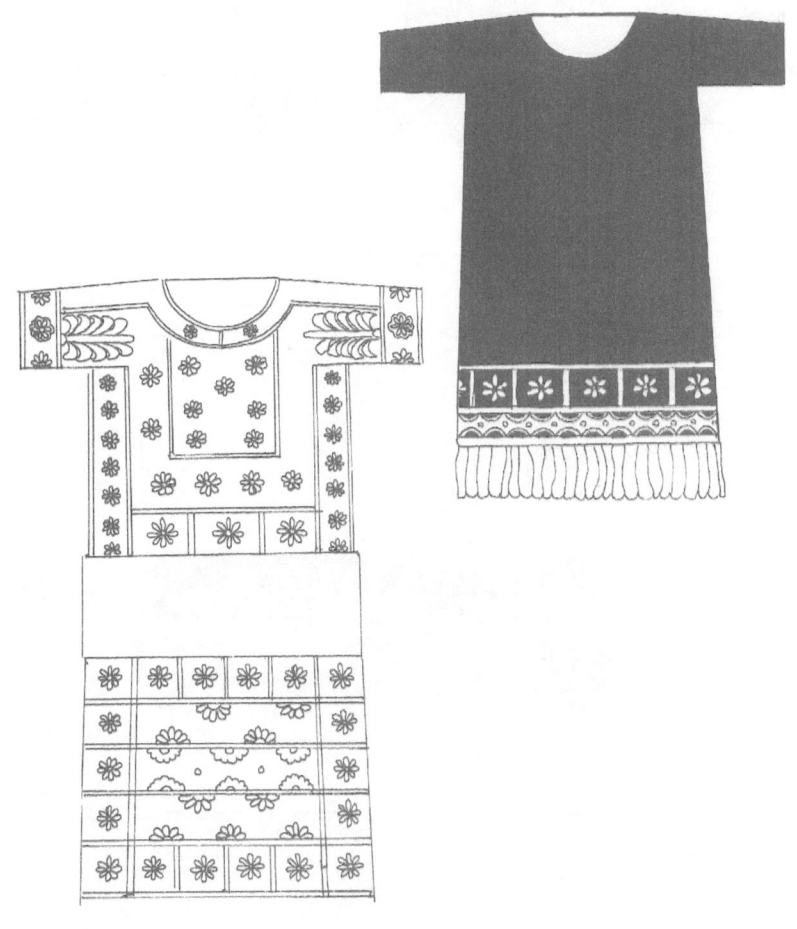

A. A sketch of a costume of the Assyrian king Tiglat-Pileser the 3rd during his campaign on the western territories.

B. A sketch of an Assyrian warrior dating to the same era.

Layard, H. I. pl. 13.

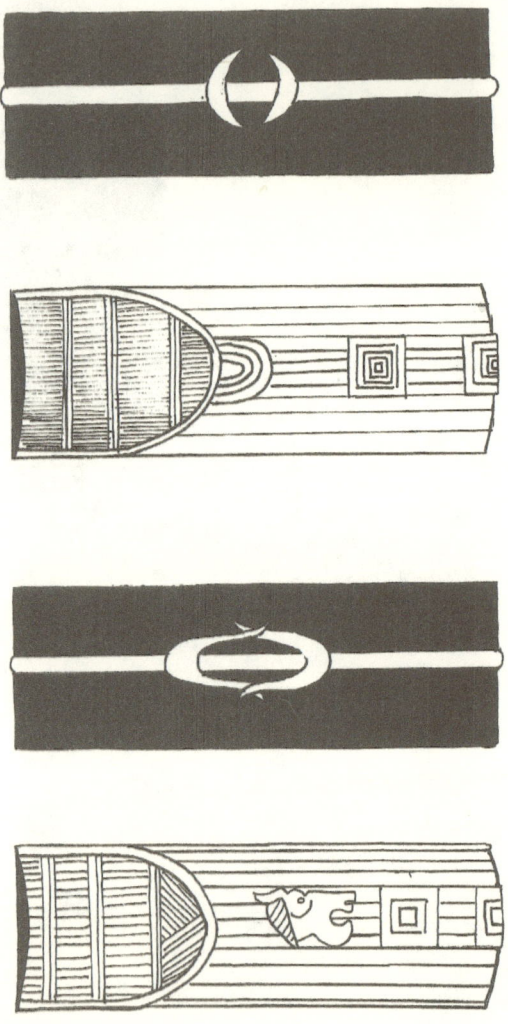

Sketches for different Assyrian belts taken from sculptures depicting complete details of their costumes.

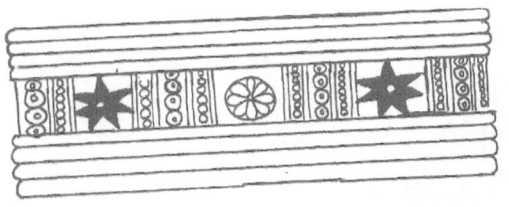

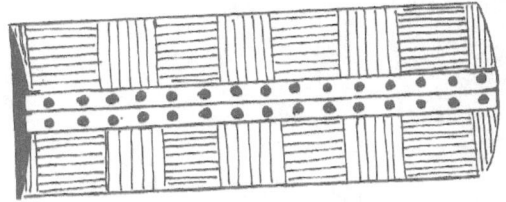

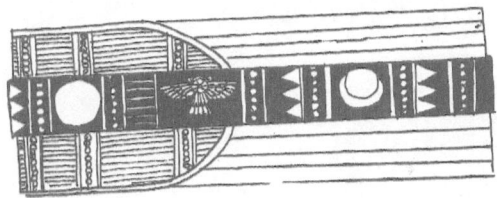

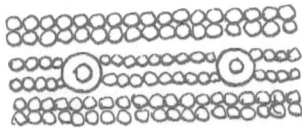

Sketches of additional belts used by Assyrians, who were known to be superb in manufacturing them, and exaggeration in decorations and coloring.

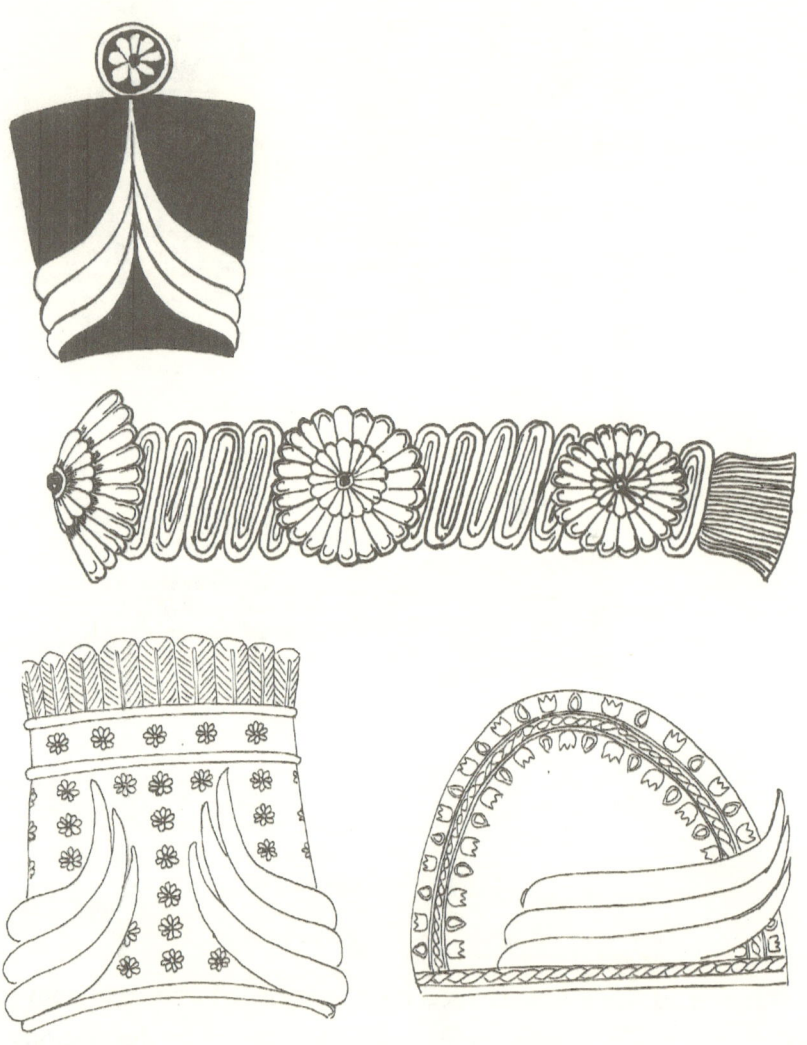

A. A sketch for a headwear of an Assyrian king.
B. The headwear of an Assyrian winged bull depicting the similarity in decorations to other costumes.
C. The headwear of a winged human god. The use of pomegranate shape as a decorative element reflects the decorative unity used by the Assyrian artists in their decorative subjects.

Layard, H. Monuments. I. pl. 38.

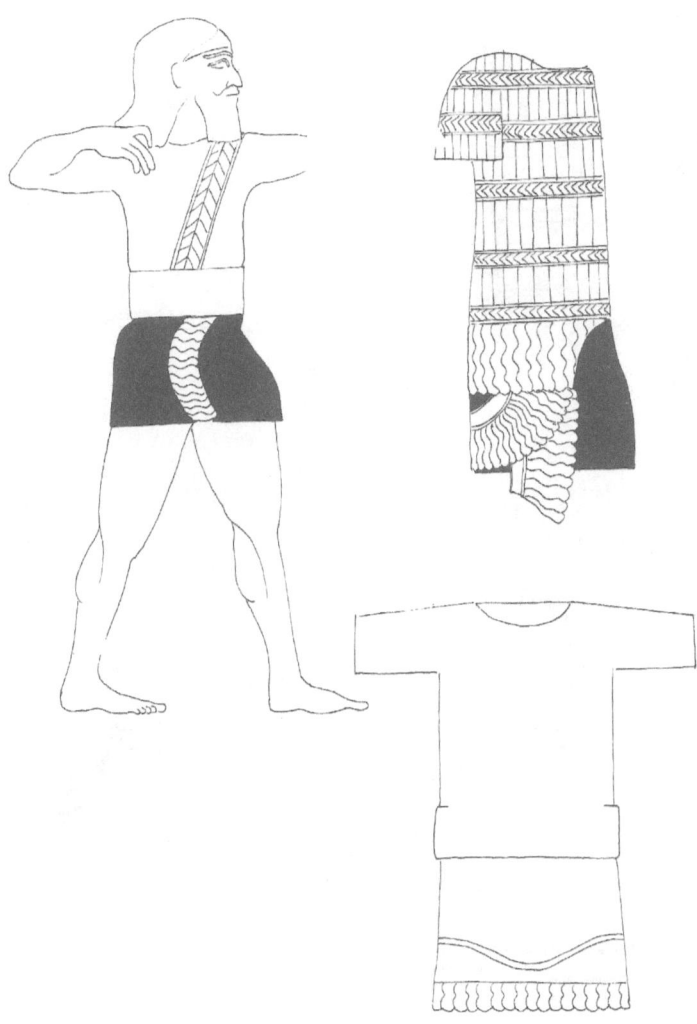

Sketches of different military outfits;

A. Short skirt and bare upper body.

B. Two- piece outfit with a tunic and a tasseled gown that ends down the belly.

C. Additional style of military outfit.

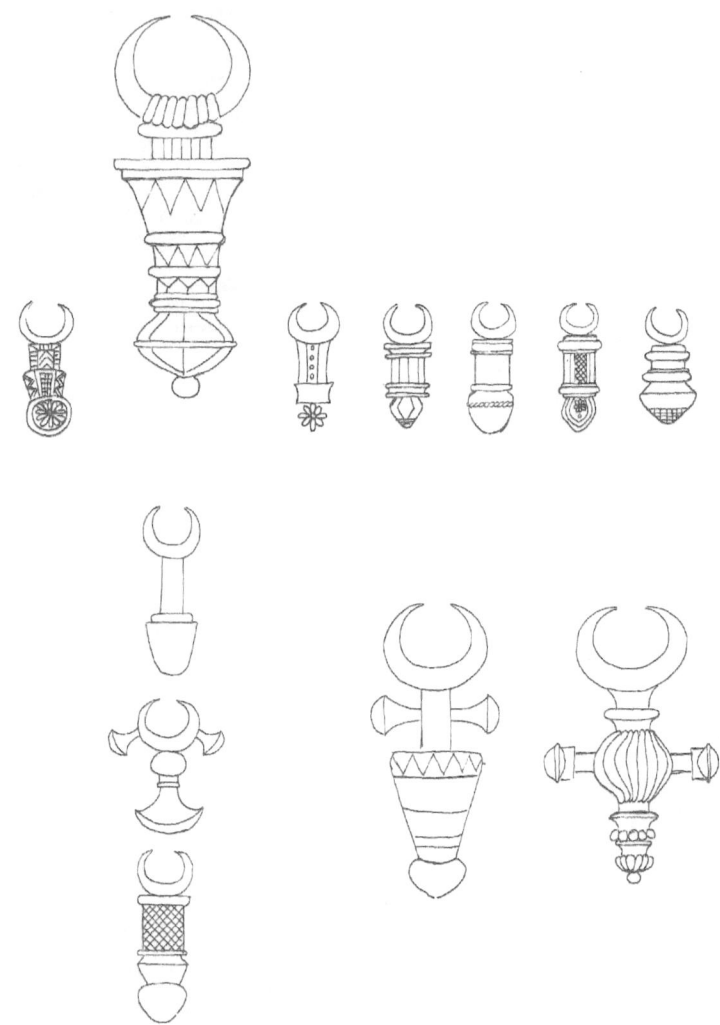

Sketches of different gold, silver, and bronze earrings found at many Assyrian sites. They varied according to the social status and the costumes worn by both males and females.

1. **Houston, M. G.**
2. **Perrot G. et ch. Chipiez.**

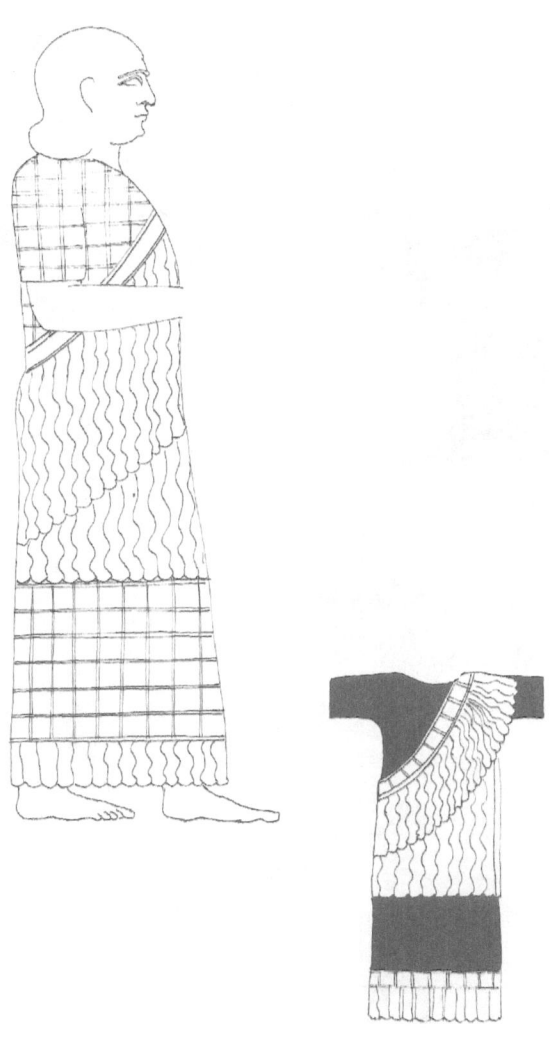

A. A sketch of another costume for a royal retinue composed of a gown decorated with adornments and a tasseled shawl.

Histoire de L'art, Tome II, pl. X.

B. A sketch of a costume for an official government employee taken from a sculpture representing the presentation of enemy prisoners to the Assyrian king.

The Sculptures of Tiglath-Pileser III. P. XXIII.

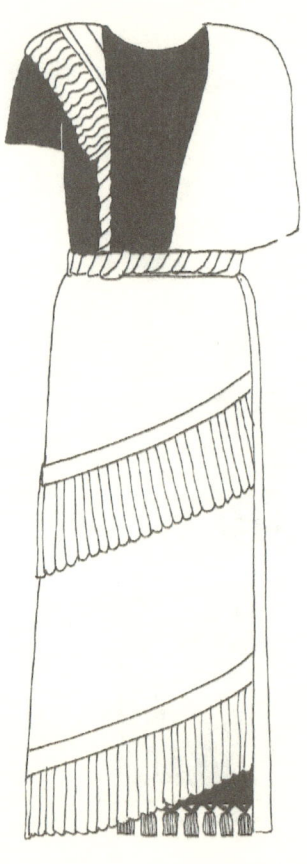
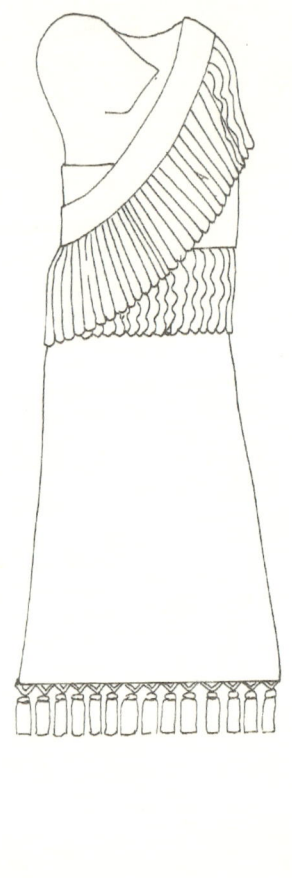

A sketch depicting different royal costumes that are based on gowns decorated with various adornments, and tasseled shawls decorated with adornments in harmony with the costumes.

Strommenger, E. The Art of Mesopotamia. Fig. 196, 196.

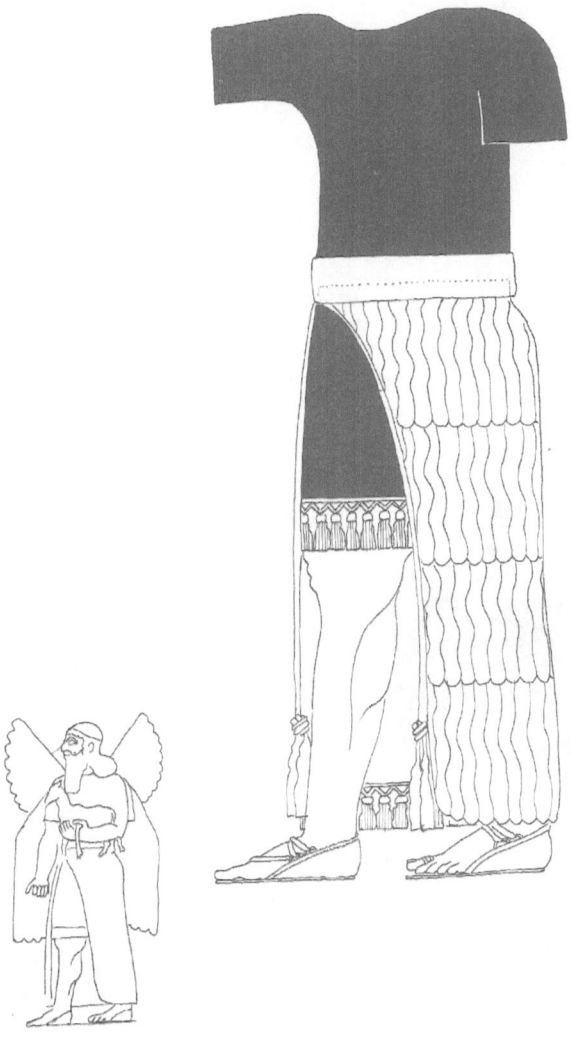

A sketch of a costume for an Assyrian winged man based on short tunic (above the knees) ending with tassels and a shawl that starts at the mid trunk. The sketch is taken fro a sculpture from Nimrud.

The Sculptures of Tiglath-Pileser III pl. CXXVI.

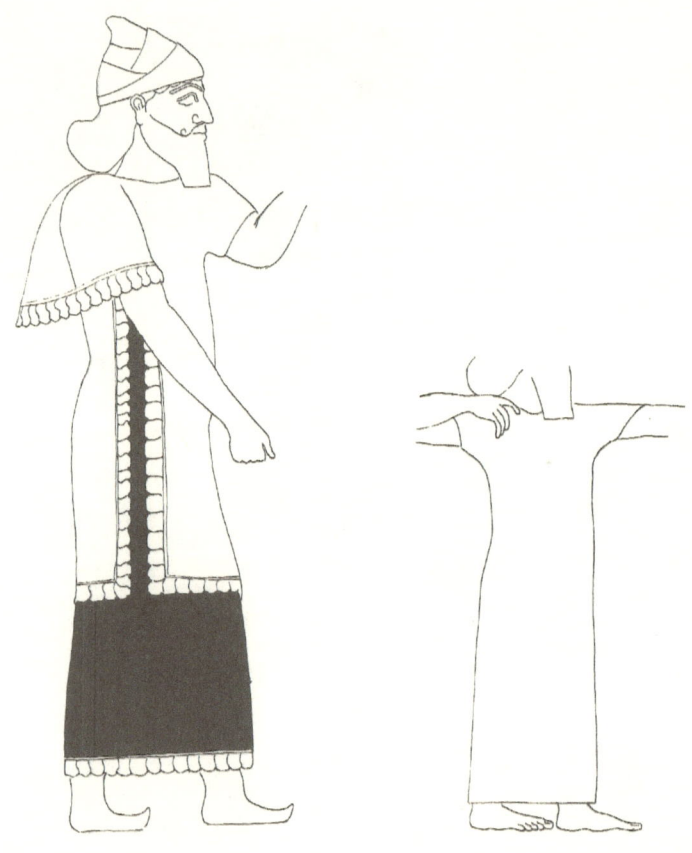

A sketch of other popular Assyrian costumes used by different social classes;

A. A clergyman in a religious ceremony. The costume is based on a tasseled tunic and gown.

B. A rare military outfit since most were short to provide flexibility in movement. Note that it is devoid of decorations.

The Sculptures of Tiglath-Pileser III, pl. XLVII, pl. LXXV.

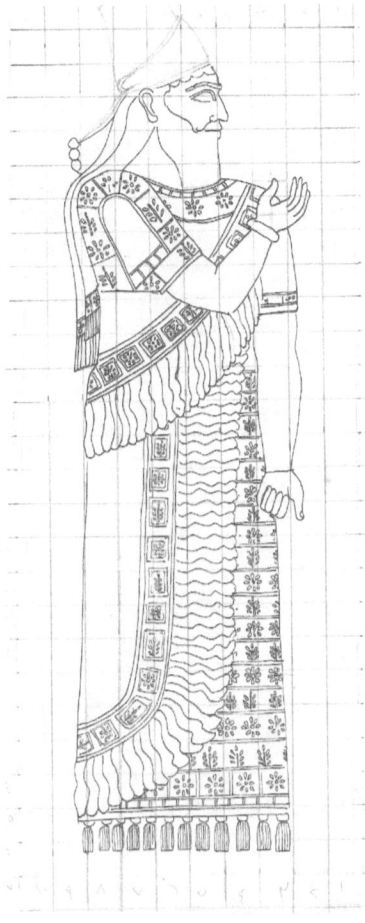

King Ashurnasirpal- 9th century BC- wearing royal costume decorated with rare adornments based on repeated plant elements. The shirt ends with tassels. The king wears a royal shawl decorated in the same manner. The sketch is taken off ivories from Nimrud.

Parrot, A. Assur. Fig. 183.

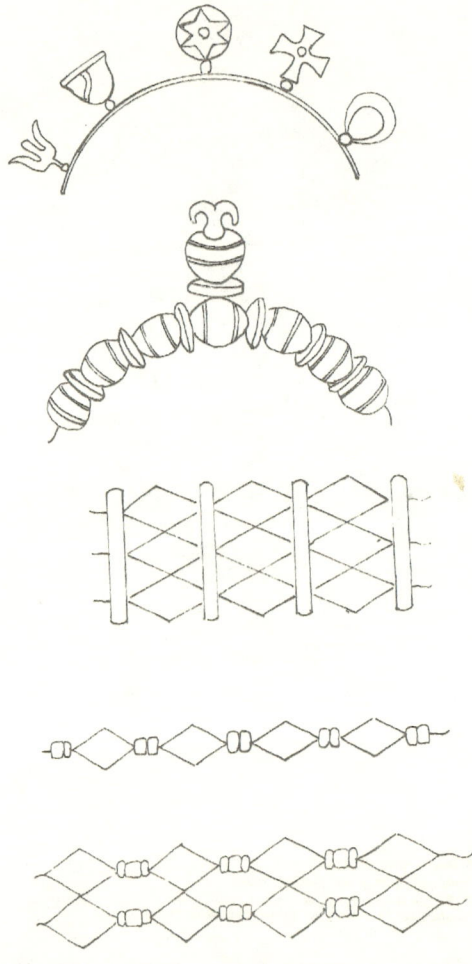

A sketch of different Assyrian necklaces used by the Assyrian king and other dignities close to the royal court.

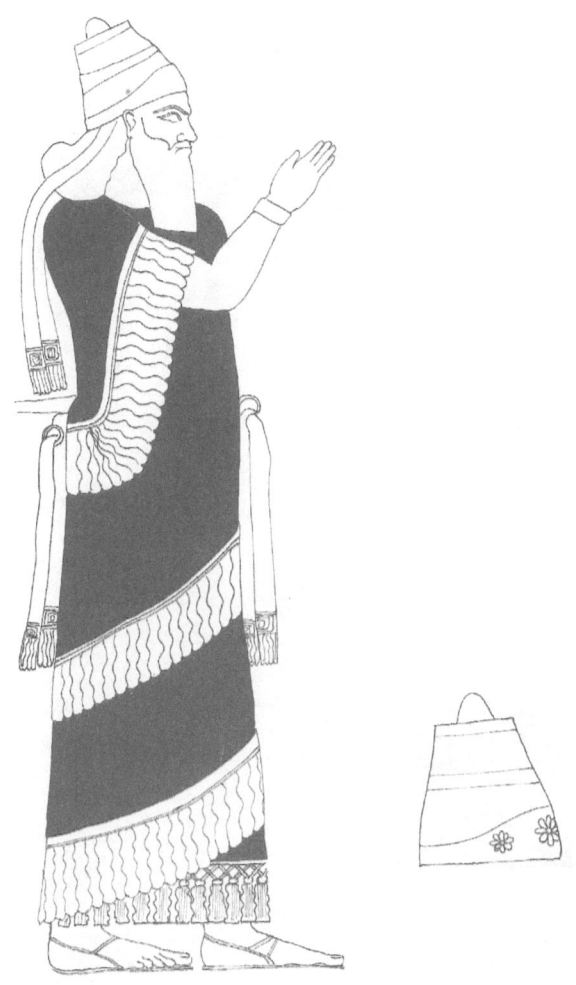

A sketch of a royal costume taken from a sculpture representing enemies pledging allegiance to the Assyrian king. The costume is based on a tasseled shawl and a long tunic ending with fringes. The royal crown is decorated with three tiers; the lower most is decorated by units in form of flowers.

The Sculptures of Tiglath-Pileser III. Pl. LXXXV.

www.ingramcontent.com/pod-product-compliance
Lightning Source LLC
Chambersburg PA
CBHW021546290526
45785CB00004BA/1747